EMOTIONAL HEALING

How to put yourself back together again

DR HARRY BARRY

First published in Great Britain in 2020 by Orion Spring
an imprint of The Orion Publishing Group Ltd
Carmelite House, 50 Victoria Embankment
London EC4Y 0DZ

An Hachette UK Company

1 3 5 7 9 10 8 6 4 2

A CIP catalogue record for this book is
available from the British Library.
ISBN (Trade paperback) 978 1 4091 8858 2
ISBN (eBook) 978 1 4091 8859 9

Typeset by Input Data Services Ltd, Somerset

Printed and bound in Great Britain by Clays Ltd, Elcograf S.p.A.

www.orionbooks.co.uk

ORION
SPRING

Whilst the amygdala in your brain controls emotions such as sadness, depression, anxiety, panic, anger or rage, grief however is better known to many of us. Harry has nailed it in one word – 'survival'. If you have lost someone special from your life, you will go to the well of *Emotional Healing*. In this book, many, many times, hope will be found there!!

Oliver Doonan, father of Anthony, who died by suicide

Emotional Healing is a refreshingly helpful book for anyone who is seeking to have a better understanding of their emotional life and wellbeing. It is written in a very simple straightforward style which makes it accessible to everyone, young or old, with or without emotional problems. It is a resource book that is full of hope. For the therapist, social worker and counsellor it is a well-researched evidence-based excellent guide for their work. And for anyone struggling with emotional problems or distress it has the potential to be a powerful self-empowering and transformative book.

Sr Stanislaus Kennedy, social campaigner, author and founder of Focus Ireland and the Sanctuary Meditation Centre

As adults we teach our young people how to understand and express their emotion, but in the absence of effective solutions, we don't teach them what to do with the emotions once they have expressed them. Harry and I have worked for years in showing people how to heal their emotional distress, leading us to happier, more fulfilling lives. In *Emotional Healing*, Harry brings the reader on this journey. Understanding the most common reasons that cause our distress but more importantly, what to do about it.

Enda Murphy, psychotherapist and author; SeeMe.ie, Supporting adults support young people

Most of us live surrounded by the turbulence of our times, often overwhelmed by its incursion into our lives. We may be brought down by the personal traumas and losses of life that affect each of us, finding our resilience and ability to cope wanting, unable to help ourselves or our families and friends. Unfortunately, most of us have grown up without learning in school or even in our families how to take care of ourselves emotionally, particularly in such situations. The strategies outlined by Dr Harry for responding to such upheavals can help us develop the emotional resilience to put ourselves 'back together again' and recover the ability to not only take care of ourselves, but those we love.

Professor Larry Culpepper, Professor of Family Medicine, Boston University School of Medicine

Dr Barry understands how we all think. He understands our emotions. These insights mean he understands how to help us heal when we feel broken. In this, his latest book, he shows in practical, sensible and helpful ways just how to do that.

Dr Fiona O'Doherty, clinical psychologist

This book is dedicated to
Anthony Doonan (1985–2014), who died
by suicide, and to his loving parents, Oliver and Anne.
&
John Ryan (1994–2014), who died by suicide, and to his loving
parents, Joe and Mary (recently deceased).

CONTENTS

PART FIVE: GRIEF

INTRODUCTION

In times of significant emotional distress, we may almost become strangers to ourselves and wonder if we will ever feel normal again. It is perfectly common to feel that you are broken or changed for ever by a difficult experience, or that you will never get over what happened. I want to reassure you that it is always possible to put yourself back together again, and I have seen it happen many times with patients in my own medical practice. As a society, we do not teach our children or ourselves about how to treat emotional distress, and yet there are so many simple and accessible tools available to us. This book will open up a door into the world of emotional healing, and show how you can access such tools.

Most of us will encounter times of significant emotional distress and will experience feelings of despair or hopelessness. In these times our emotional world is in turmoil. We may feel broken inside as life, with all of its vicissitudes, comes calling. It is highly likely that you have already experienced such periods of emotional upheaval, or perhaps you are in the middle of one right now. It comes to us all.

However badly you are feeling at this moment in time, the good news is that by applying many of the insights and concepts in this book to your life, you can learn to recover, grow and thrive as a human being.

We rarely talk about the importance of emotional distress in our lives. There is a current cultural obsession with mental health and mental illness, but far less discussion of the experience of emotional distress. Mental health and mental illness (which relate in general to bouts of schizophrenia, bipolar disorder, severe treatment-resistant depression, anorexia nervosa and severe OCD) are self-explanatory. But perhaps the greatest threat to your mental health and peace of mind emanates from the world of emotional distress. The triggers for such distress may vary from person to person. They may relate to loss, relationship difficulties, work or financial pressures, bullying, traumatic events or adverse childhood experiences, to name but a few. Sometimes it is simpler to group them under one heading – life.

I have always believed that, for most of us, life is tough, unyielding, unfair, even brutal. Many of you will empathize with this statement! For life, although a source of wonder, joy and beauty, is also hard. It is filled with periods of sadness, anxiety, depression, hurt, shame, guilt, emotional pain, loss, loneliness and, on occasions, even hopelessness and despair. In general, if you are emotionally distressed as a result of any of the above, you are *not* mentally unwell or ill. You are simply struggling to understand and cope with the impact on your life of some powerful negative emotions.

Can you survive such periods and learn to thrive? Can you put yourself together again, and if so, how? Is it possible to piece together the often-complex emotional jigsaw of life when it becomes splintered? To make sense of how you feel when emotionally distressed? To learn how to recognise and manage your emotions? To feel whole again? To be at peace with yourself and life? To achieve emotional healing?

Introduction

I believe that you can indeed put yourself together again following such periods of emotional turmoil and distress. Emotional healing is available to us all. It does not require months or years of working with 'experts' to achieve such an objective. It involves developing an understanding of how you work and what works for you. Nowhere will this be more apparent, for example, than when we explore the world of grief, a universal experience which affects us all so differently.

This book is not designed for (but hopefully might assist) those experiencing a bout of mental illness. Rather, it is a healing guide to managing bouts of emotional distress.

Some struggle to understand the distinction between these concepts. As mentioned above, mental illness relates to conditions such as schizophrenia, treatment-resistant depression or bipolar disorder. These often have a strong underlying biological basis, and may require specialist care, medication and, on occasions, inpatient care.

Emotional distress, by contrast, relates more to our emotional reactions to periods where we find ourselves struggling to cope with difficult life experiences.

On our journey throughout this book, I will introduce you to some wonderful people struggling with bouts of significant emotional distress, and together we will discover how they achieved emotional healing. In order to protect the confidentiality of patients, I have chosen to create composite characters to represent common situations that I have come across in my practice.

Our journey towards emotional healing will focus primarily on understanding and altering the principal unhealthy, negative emotions underlying emotional distress, recognising and altering unhelpful thinking patterns, and managing our behavioural responses to these often-overwhelming emotions.

You may find yourself drawn to the section of the book that feels of greatest relevance to you. Feel free to go directly to any particular chapter, but you will find the chapters build on each other, and you may find helpful techniques in other chapters. By the end of the book, it's my hope that you will have developed a deeper insight into the world of emotional healing, and how you can apply it to your own life.

The great message of hope is that there is light at the end of the tunnel, no matter how emotionally distressed you are, or how black life may seem. You have the power within you to navigate a passage out of the darkness and into the light. You have the power to heal yourself. Read on and learn how to do just that.

PART ONE

Emotional Healing

1. What Is Emotional Healing?

The objective of this book is to assist you in your journey towards inner peace and calm, regardless of the circumstances of your life. Emotional healing will help you discover within yourself the deep emotional reserves which allow us to cope when periods of emotional distress arise. But firstly, it is important to define what we mean by emotional healing.

Emotional healing relates to a two-fold process whereby you learn to:

1 Identify your emotional responses to any distressing negative experience, situation or trauma which has occurred in your life, as well as the thinking, perceptions and beliefs underlying such emotions, and finally the unhealthy behavioural patterns which can result from them.
2 Tap into your inner reserves to reshape these thoughts, emotions and behaviours, with the goal of self-healing.

It is clear that such an approach requires us as human beings to become increasingly self-aware. Whilst this may seem to be a simple matter, many of us fall at the first hurdle, namely identifying our emotions.

What Are Our Emotions?

Emotions are powerfully intense feelings or sensations which can be triggered by conscious or unconscious events. They are intimately connected to our thoughts and behaviours and play a major role in our lives. They also, if we pay attention, form useful signposts into what is going on in our interior world, both conscious and unconscious.

Emotions relate to how we feel and usually last for relatively short durations, usually minutes to hours. If these emotions last for longer periods – hours or perhaps days – we call them moods. Emotions can be positive or negative, and healthy or unhealthy.

Positive emotions include joy, happiness, pleasure, love, awe, trust, contentment and peacefulness. We call these emotions positive because they make us feel good about ourselves and give us a sense of wellbeing.

Healthy negative emotions such as sadness help us cope with the many difficulties which life throws at us, such as loss. A healthy negative emotion such as sadness is still uncomfortable but it is helpful as it allows us to sit with and attempt to come to terms with some loss in our lives. Remorse is another common example of a healthy negative emotion, which may lead us away from future behaviour that will cause us to feel regret.

Unhealthy negative emotions, however, often impede us in dealing with such difficulties. We classify depression as an unhealthy negative emotion, for example, as it makes us feel bad about ourselves, which may result in unhealthy behaviours such as isolating ourselves from others. Another classic example of an unhealthy negative emotion is hurt, where our natural behavioural response is to become hypersensitive or extremely irritable if we believe that we are being treated unfairly.

Emotions are often associated with physical symptoms – fear may give us sensations such as palpitations, a dry mouth, or difficulty taking deep breaths. Anger may mean clenched muscles or tension headaches. Both sadness and its *alter ego* joy can trigger tears. Hurt and rejection may be associated with a deep-seated sensation of pain.

When we describe emotions as 'feelings', there is often an unstated suggestion that these physical symptoms will be present – we feel the emotion in the body itself. And indeed the current neurobiological understanding of emotions supports the physical manifestation of feelings.

Emotions are also intimately connected to behaviour. If fearful or anxious, we may use avoidant or safety behaviour. If depressed, we may withdraw socially or become intensely self-critical. If ashamed, we will avoid contact with people and situations that might trigger any potential for others to judge us. If hurt, we may become hypersensitive or irritable. If angry, we may lash out verbally or physically.

Emotions are also completely interwoven with our thoughts, both conscious and unconscious. This is increasingly seen as a two-way conversation, at both a neuroscientific and practical everyday level. So, our thoughts can both trigger certain emotions and also modify or modulate them. Learning to work with this modification and modulation of thoughts and emotions is the secret to emotional healing.

The Neuroscience of Emotions

A whole body of research has explored the role of the brain in emotions. Leading world experts such as Richard Davidson, Joseph Le Doux, Anthony Damasio and many others have explored the subject. It is not possible to go into the subject in depth here, but the essential principles are key to emotional healing, and it is helpful to have a basic understanding of them.

It is useful but by no means essential to understand the neuroscience underlying emotions. But because some of the names and concepts will appear throughout the book, I do recommend a quick perusal of the information below.

(a) Emotions are generated primarily but not exclusively within one of the oldest parts of the brain called the limbic system, an evolutionary relic of our dinosaur past. This part of the brain developed somewhere between 150 and 300 million years ago, as a follow-on to the earlier, more primitive reptilian brain which came into being around 300 to 500 million years ago. It has multiple functions, such as monitoring and controlling our internal body temperature, blood pressure, bodily hormones and internal circadian rhythms. Alongside monitoring these vital bodily functions, one of its other primary functions is to oversee our emotional world, which is why it is frequently referred to as the emotional brain. This is the area of the brain which produces key emotions such as anxiety, panic, anger, depression, sadness, disgust, hurt and emotional pain.

(b) Two key structures within the limbic system are the amygdala and the hippocampus. The amygdala is seen as the mother and father of most of our emotions, especially sadness, depression, anxiety, panic, anger, frustration, rage and so on. The hippocampus is where we organize and distribute our contextual memories of the day. The amygdala and the hippocampus work hand in hand. If I am watching a sad film, the hippocampus will assist in the storage of the contextual element of the film, what it was about and where I watched it. The amygdala on the other hand will store the memory of my emotional reactions – in this case, sadness.

(c) Our emotional world is carefully monitored and modulated by the pre-frontal cortex, situated at the front of the brain and seen as the rational, sensible, problem-solving part of the brain.

(d) There are lightning-fast connections between each of these key areas of the brain, involved in both the generation and regulation of our emotions. This explains why we can so easily shift from being calm and happy in the morning to being anxious and fretful in the afternoon, depending on what is going on in our lives during that particular day.

(e) Many of these organs which generate emotions also trigger internal hormonal and physical reactions in your body. Your amygdala, for example, oversees your stress system and if you are panicky it will send information to your adrenal stress gland to produce the fear hormone adrenaline. If you are angry or frustrated, it will trigger the aggression hormone noradrenaline. If you feel anxious or depressed, it may trigger surges of the chronic stress hormone glucocortisol. This explains the physical symptoms which we all are so aware of when experiencing such emotions. We will be mentioning these in greater detail later.

f) Finally, it is worth noting that some experts, such as Richard Davidson, have discovered that when you are working more out of the right side of the brain, you are increasingly likely to experience negative unhealthy emotions such as anxiety or depression. While working more out of the left side of the brain tends to make you joyful, calmer and positive.

Identifying Your Emotions

For decades, I have marvelled at how difficult it can be to identify your emotions. I frequently ask patients, 'How did this event make you feel?', only to be met with an uncomfortable silence. We are often unsure as to how we feel. There are many reasons for this difficulty. Although emotions rule our lives, we often feel strangely uncomfortable reflecting on or discussing them. In my clinical experience, men especially struggle to identify or accept their emotions.

What is an Emotional Menu?

When faced with a distressed person who is unable to articulate how they feel emotionally, one of the first things I do is offer them an 'emotional menu', where I give them a pre-written list of healthy and unhealthy negative emotions to choose from. This is because it is often difficult for patients, especially if very distressed, to recognise or name for themselves the relevant emotions which they may be experiencing.

Unhealthy negative emotions may include:
- Anxiety
- Depression
- Hurt
- Anger
- Shame
- Guilt
- Frustration

Healthy negative emotions may include:
- Concern
- Sadness
- Remorse
- Regret
- Disappointment
- Annoyance

I then ask the patient to choose the emotions underlying their distress at that moment. Identifying these emotions for the first time can be a life-changing experience, giving clarity to a situation that may have felt overwhelmingly confusing.

The patient can then focus on their unhealthy negative emotions, which I suggest they list in order of importance. I explain to them that emotions are the signposts to our inner world and can greatly assist in exploring their thoughts and behaviours. Learning how to create such a menu is a crucial first step towards acquiring emotional healing.

The Emotional Menu Exercise

At this stage, I would like to ask you to carry out the following exercise, where you learn how to create your own emotional menu.

1. For the next four weeks I want you to carry a notebook and whenever something distresses you, write down the triggering event. Let's take an example where you develop a sudden phobia to using the lift at work. You would write down the triggering event as follows:

    'I went to use the lift at work and felt that I couldn't breathe properly. I had to get out immediately.'

2. Then use the menu laid out above as a guide to explore which emotions were triggered. Were you feeling anxious, depressed, hurt, frustrated or simply sad or annoyed? Identify the following emotions.

    'The emotions I experienced which were triggered by the lift were fear, and frustration and annoyance with myself for not being able to use the lift.'

3. If several emotions are triggered, I suggest you should list them in order of importance to you, at that moment.

    'Fear was the primary emotion, followed by frustration and annoyance.'

4. Pay special attention to your unhealthy negative emotions.

    'The unhealthy negative emotions in this case were fear and frustration.'

5. Do not be concerned how to interpret or manage your emotions. It is just important, at this stage, to identify them.

The more you perform this exercise, the more accurately you will begin to identify your emotions. This is an important first step towards learning how best to emotionally heal yourself when you feel distressed. If you can identify your emotional responses to the cause of your present difficulties, then coping with them becomes easier. This exercise also demonstrates how often several emotions are triggered by the same situation. Learning to identify which emotions are involved when you are exposed to such situations also removes confusion. You can now identify emotionally why you are so distressed. If you are struggling, however, to even identify how you are feeling emotionally, it becomes harder to self-heal.

I cannot overemphasise the importance of this first step. It can be incredibly empowering and liberating to identify individual emotions and write them down on paper. It is like opening a door into what was previously a 'locked-away' space in the deeper recesses of your mind. It does not necessarily mean that shining a light into such spaces makes coping with what you might find any easier, but this first step will greatly assist you to achieve your objective of healing inner pain and finding true peace.

Healing

Now that we have explored the world of emotions, let's turn our attention to the word 'healing'. This is one of the most used, if frequently misunderstood, terms in physical and mental health. The word 'heal' comes from the Old English word *'haelan'*, which means to cure or make whole again. Healing is the process of restoring a healthy mind or body following a period of distress or illness. It is traditionally associated with physical illness, whether related to infection, trauma, cancer or some other bodily ailment. 'Healing' suggests that we are no longer experiencing significant pain or distress from the underlying ailment or condition and can return to normal functioning in our everyday lives. Medicine and nursing are often described as the 'healing professions' as they assist in this process.

Modern medicine has advanced more in the past fifty years (especially in the past decade) than in the previous ten thousand years. We can now heal many physical illnesses that were once seen as untreatable. It is predicted that over the next three decades we will make vast strides towards healing the major illnesses, such as some forms of cancer, spinal-cord injuries and many neuro-degenerative conditions, such as dementia, presently considered untreatable.

But human beings are not simply physical entities. We also have a psychological (and in the eyes of some, a spiritual) dimension which can be affected by illness or distress. It is only in the past fifty years, especially in the past few decades, that mental or psychological ailments have been accepted as being of equal importance to physical ones.

From the earliest times, there were always individuals who were seen by other members of their communities or tribes as 'healers'. In most cases, such healing was holistic in nature. It involved healing the body, mind and in some cases the spirit of the person in distress, as a whole. Traditional healers would not have simply treated a symptom on its own, but as part of something greater. Many of these healers were revered within their communities and sometimes seen as having 'special powers'.

There has always been a difference between the West and the East in terms of how medicine and healing were perceived. With the advent of modern medicine and the multitude of discoveries over the past fifty years, the West has come down strongly in favour of a scientific, data-backed approach to healing. This has led to an increasing tendency to break the person down from a whole being into a collection of different organs and physical structures. The cardiologist manages heart conditions, the respiratory physician takes on illnesses affecting the lungs, the neurologist deals with illnesses affecting the brain and so on. This has led, in turn, to the gradual demoting of the 'whole person' in the eyes of modern medicine.

The East has tended to approach healing in a different way and many of the 'traditional' healing approaches evolved in China, Japan and Tibet. These incorporated therapies aimed at the total person – mind, body and spirit.

Over time, both Eastern and Western cultures have absorbed positive healing messages from each other, whilst retaining strong elements of their own approaches.

When it comes to emotional healing, and physical healing too, I encourage a holistic element, where we view the person in their entirety.

For the purposes of our discussion, we shall be approaching the concept of healing in a holistic manner. This will involve initially discovering the causes of the person's distress and how this is affecting them emotionally and viscerally, leading on to exploring what negative behaviours (if any) are present and how we can change them. It will also involve an exploration of the thinking patterns underlying such emotions and behaviours.

It is clearly beyond the scope of this book to explore the world of spiritual healing, so I will be primarily focusing on the physical and psychological rather than venturing into the world of philosophy and spirituality. Each person must decide on their own path in such areas. There can be little doubt, however, that for emotional healing to be effective it must involve changes to the essence of who we are. Allow yourself to explore whatever brings you comfort in difficult times.

When Emotional Distress Arrives

Life can on occasions be difficult, as most of us can attest to. Loss, hurt, conflict, confusion, misunderstandings and trauma are realities frequently interwoven throughout all of our lives. Thankfully such periods will also be interspersed with moments of joy, laughter, happiness and periods of peace and contentment.

In modern life there seems to be a belief that we should be happy all the time, or at least in pursuit of happiness. And that may lead us to feel that we have failed in some way if we are feeling sad or distressed. But the truth lies somewhere in the middle – no one can be happy all the time, and sadness and emotional turmoil are simply part of life. Whilst the concept of constant happiness is wonderful in theory, in practice it is both unhealthy and impractical to spend our lives trying to achieve it as a permanent state.

All of us therefore will experience times when our peace and calm is broken. Where life with all its travails arrives. It is at such times that you may experience bouts of emotional distress. It is important that we use the term 'bout' when discussing emotional distress. You may be assuming that the distressing emotions which you are at present experiencing are always going to be your lot, even if, as we will discover later, this is not the case. Emotional distress tends to come in bouts of varying length and intensity. The good news is that such bouts tend to give way to periods of calm, especially if you have developed skills to manage your emotional distress.

When hiding down in the 'bunker' during such periods, however with the 'artillery shells of life' raining in upon you, it can be difficult to visualize life ever returning to normal. Yet with time the bombardment will cease, hostilities will end, peace and calm will be restored, and you can once again enjoy the normal, simple joys of life.

Sometimes when immersed in a bout of significant emotional distress, especially if the difficulties are present for some time, it can be difficult to believe that this is just a 'bout' or 'phase of life'. You may doubt that you can navigate your way through it and find yourself on the other side. It is worth writing down daily in a diary, during such periods, the following statement: 'This, too, shall pass'. It may sound trite, but it is important to remind yourself that these feelings are transient. Over time, this saying will become your new mantra, and it will inspire you to keep going.

There is an important message here. No matter how difficult a period of time you are having, or how emotionally distressed you are feeling, with the application of some of the ideas explored in this book, you can learn to emotionally self-heal, and even build resilience to prepare for future episodes.

This is especially important if you are becoming increasingly hopeless and despairing, and find yourself considering suicide to end such pain. How many who have travelled down that road, only to survive, have subsequently rejoiced that they were unsuccessful! Survivors regularly observe how, when caught up in their emotional distress, they had failed to comprehend that the bout would pass, circumstances would change, and they would find themselves eventually healed. For this reason, some call suicide a 'permanent solution to a temporary problem'.

If you do find yourself in this space, it is essential that you reach out and talk to someone. There may be a close friend or family member you can trust. Perhaps you can relate to your family doctor or a clergyman. It may be that a therapist can help best. Or it may be someone at the end of a phone helpline, who is there to simply listen. At the back of this book are numbers you can contact. You owe it to yourself and those you love to find a different route out of your current – and temporary – bout of emotional pain and distress.

When Do We Need Emotional Healing?

In my work, I have met many wonderful people who have enriched my understanding of what it truly means to be human. They have shared their life stories with me and told of how their peace of mind felt as if it was destroyed by a multitude of what they viewed as negative life experiences.

Some of them, whilst distressed by such experiences, are able to be resilient; understanding, perhaps, even in the middle of their turmoil, that the experience is temporary. Others are really struggling, carrying large burdens of guilt, hurt, shame or grief, for example, and finding themselves persistently distressed. This is the group that may require a root-and-branch approach to assist themselves to self-heal.

How can you tell if you are struggling? Consider the following questions:

- Does it feel as if life is crushing you, or pulling you down into a negative vortex?
- Are you finding it difficult to see a path out of your current difficulties?
- Are you are carrying emotional burdens such as shame, guilt or grief?
- Is your emotional pain or distress interfering with aspects of your life such as personal or family relationships, or work?

If you answered 'yes' to any of these questions, then it is time to discover new ways to self-heal. If you find yourself heading down dark roads and cannot see a reason to continue, then it is definitely time to join us on a voyage of discovery into the world of emotional self-healing.

Because no matter how emotionally distressed you are or what dark place you are currently residing in, there is a path out of that dark maze. I have assisted countless people on that path and rejoiced when they, through the power of their own minds, came to a state of emotional healing.

How Do I Manage a Bout of Emotional Distress?

If you find yourself currently emotionally distressed, or have experienced such feelings in the past and would like to equip yourself for the future, it is essential to learn and practise a structured approach as to how best to deal with them. Otherwise you may experience long periods of such distress.

For the rest of this chapter I am going to lay out the structured approach I have discovered, which, over many years of practice, has transformed the lives of those experiencing such bouts. The first and most important element of such an approach is to explore such issues '*on paper*' in an organized, pragmatic, structured manner, '*in your own handwriting*'.

There is a great power in seeing the issues which are causing you such emotional distress in your mind dissected on paper in your own handwriting. It makes both the issues involved and your response to them real, rather than the ramblings of your emotional mind. It allows you to identify and rationalise your own emotions, getting them out of your emotional mind whilst allowing your rational mind the opportunity to problem-solve the issues involved.

Such an approach is backed up by current understanding as to how the brain works.

As mentioned earlier, each one of us has a rational brain and an emotional brain and there are continuous conversations happening between both. But the emotional brain has the edge as we tend to think and behave emotionally rather than rationally, especially when our negative emotions are being triggered by difficult experiences. The emotional brain has an inherent capacity to overrun and swamp information emanating from the rational brain. Understanding this is the secret to understanding emotional distress. This tendency of the emotional brain, when in a negative mode, to overpower and dominate the rational brain is also an essential ingredient in anxiety, depression and especially self-harm and suicide. In such circumstances our normal ability to think and behave sensibly or logically is sidelined. The internal voices in our emotional mind tend to take over and silence our rational or pragmatic mind. Often these internal voices, which can be hypercritical, begin to reverberate over and over relentlessly in a process we call 'rumination', which we will be discussing later.

When you are emotionally distressed, whatever the triggering event is, the emotional brain and mind may take control and such circular ruminations can become the norm. A typical example of such ruminations occurs in depression, where you may experience circular thoughts (especially if awake in the middle of the night) such as 'I am worthless', 'People would be better off avoiding me', 'I am a failure', 'The world would be a better place without me'. None of these thoughts are true of course. Yet you are unable to either switch them off or challenge them in your emotional mind.

To counteract this tendency, you must harness other areas of the brain to challenge these distressing ramblings emanating from the emotional brain. We do this by writing down *on paper* the details of what is troubling you, how it is affecting you, why this is the case, what behaviours are contributing to your difficulties and how you could change things for the better. This allows your rational, logical brain, which loves seeing things written down in front of it, to pragmatically carve through and problem-solve issues. It doesn't make the emotional distress any easier but does provide a vehicle to manage it. And it is a reminder that *you are not your thoughts*.

There is something intensely personal, liberating and challenging about seeing this information that you have provided in your own handwriting on a page in front of your eyes. It is 'you' writing down real information about 'you' and where you find yourself at that moment in time – not some vague ramblings emanating from your emotional mind.

I would now like to briefly elaborate on a therapy approach which allows you to put down on paper, in such a structured manner, issues that are causing your emotional distress and to subsequently analyse them. We will be using this approach throughout this book and will demonstrate how it has powerfully assisted so many people to self-heal.

Cognitive Behaviour Therapy

Cognitive Behaviour Therapy, or CBT, is based on two simple but profound concepts: first, that our thoughts influence our emotions, which influence behaviour, so what we think affects what we feel and do; and second, that it is not what happens to us in life that matters, but how we choose to interpret it.

The person credited with transforming the way in which we link thoughts, emotions and behaviours is the great psychotherapist and father of CBT, Albert Ellis.

I was introduced to CBT and especially the world of Ellis by leading CBT therapist and trainer Enda Murphy. He imbued in myself and many others a great love and understanding of Ellis and his amazing insights and techniques. Enda's book *5 Steps to Happiness* (visit www.SeeMe.ie) details many of these insights.

Ellis's genius was to highlight what had been known for thousands of years: 'It is not what happens to us in life that upsets us and causes us so much grief, but rather how we interpret it.' He also believed that our interpretation of events, which can cause us so much pain, was based on simple inbuilt belief systems that we developed as human beings mainly due to our experiences in childhood. He called these belief systems Rational and Irrational Beliefs. These belief systems, as will be explored in more detail later, play a major role in how we think about and manage our responses to emotionally distressing situations.

To link our thoughts, emotions and behavioural responses to situations or events in our lives, Ellis came up with the following simple ABC model.

A

'A' stands for 'activating event'. This is an event that sets up a certain chain of thoughts, emotions and behaviours. It can refer to an external event – either present or future – or an internal one, such as a memory, mental image, thought or dream. A useful way of examining the activating event is to divide it into the 'trigger', the actual event that starts the ball rolling, and the 'inference' we assign to that trigger – how we view the event.

A good example might be where you are due to sit an exam about which you are anxious. Your trigger in this case would be the exam and the inference would be that you might fail the exam and that, if this happened, you would consider yourself to be a failure.

B

'B' stands for 'belief', an all-encompassing term which includes our thoughts; our demands on ourselves, the world and others; our attitudes; and the meaning we attach to internal and external events in our lives. It is through our beliefs that we assess and interpret triggers. These beliefs can be Rational or Irrational.

In the example given above, your belief might take the form of an absolute demand that 'I must not fail my exam and if I do, I am a failure'.

C

'C' stands for 'consequences', an all-inclusive term which can include emotional and physical experiences, and especially the behavioural responses that result from A and B.

In the example above, your emotion would be anxiety, the physical responses might be fatigue, muscle tension, stomach in knots, difficulty sleeping, etc. Your behaviour might be considering trying to avoid the exam or overpreparing for it. Or perhaps eating poorly or drinking excess alcohol to cope with your anxiety.

At the heart of Ellis's model lies the world of rational and irrational beliefs. He believed that all of us develop such beliefs, which we picked up like viruses when passing through childhood, adolescence and young adult life.

Rational beliefs were sensible and logical and led to healthy negative emotions such as sadness. Irrational beliefs, on the other hand, were destructive, unhelpful and often completely illogical and led to unhealthy negative emotions such as shame and guilt, for example.

Ellis also believed that it is through these beliefs that we interpret everything that happens to us in life. Nowhere is this more relevant than in the management of emotional distress.

He noted that our irrational beliefs led to absolute, impossible to achieve demands on ourselves, which in turn led us to become emotionally distressed and to behave accordingly. In the exam example above I may irrationally believe that I must be able to control all of the variables which doing an exam can induce (the questions on the paper, whether I am sick or unwell on the day, the state of mind of the person marking it, etc.) and demand that I 'must' pass it. It is this impossible demand, emanating from the belief that I can somehow control all aspects of life, which leads me to become anxious in the first place. We will be exploring this in greater detail later.

The great strength of using Ellis's ABC model is that it allows you to simply analyse on paper those situations and events which are causing your emotional difficulties. This helps unveil where your thinking and behaviours may be blocking you from dealing with the situation and thus causing you to remain emotionally distressed. Later we will demonstrate how you can learn to challenge and reshape such thinking and behaviours.

Ellis's ABC Model in Action

Let us meet Mary, who has developed a phobia about using lifts.

Her ABC, written down in her own handwriting, might look like this.

A – Activating Event:
  • Trigger: getting into a lift
  Inference/danger: I am going to become physically extremely anxious; I might collapse or struggle to breathe;

I might die; I might lose control and go crazy; others might see me if this happens and judge me.

B – Belief/Demands:

- 'I must not be exposed to any situation (e.g. lift) where I become extremely physically anxious.'

C – Consequences:

- Emotional reactions: panic
- Physical reactions: stomach in knots, shaking, sweating, heart pounding, fast breathing, dry mouth, muscle tension, a sense of dread
- Behaviour: avoid lifts

The great advantage that Mary now has in examining her ABC is that she possesses a clear picture of what it is about getting into a lift that is causing her to become so distressed. It now becomes much easier for her to develop techniques to banish this and indeed any other phobias out of her life. We will be returning to her story later to see how she does just that.

We will also be calling on the services of Dr Jim, a GP who specialises in using CBT approaches to achieve emotional healing.

The ABC system allows us to identify in a structured manner which emotions are distressing us, the irrational thinking patterns underlying them and the negative physical and behavioural consequences of the emotion in question. This in turn allows us to challenge and change any unhelpful thought processes or behaviours that are uncovered. We will see how this process evolves throughout the rest of this book.

It has been my experience as a GP for the past thirty-five years that the vast majority of those who have come to me for assistance with emotional distress will be suffering from one or more of six unhealthy negative emotions (anxiety, depression, shame, guilt, hurt and anger) or are struggling with grief. Grief, contrary to popular opinion, is not an emotion but rather relates to the process of how we deal with loss.

We begin our journey by exploring two of the most common unhealthy negative emotions, namely anxiety and depression.

PART TWO

Anxiety and Depression

2. Anxiety

Would you like to be free of panic attacks for ever? And develop techniques to eliminate those distressing feelings of fear and panic when exposed to certain situations such as lifts, planes, crowded areas or shopping centres, or perhaps coming in contact with specific animals or insects? Would you like to manage the gnawing anxiety which may be filling your life with foreboding and constant worrying? Or learn how to overcome those feelings of anxiety which you may experience when having to socially interact with others? If the answer to any of these questions is yes, then this chapter is for you.

Over decades of assisting people with emotional distress, the commonest underlying unhealthy negative emotion I encountered was anxiety, along with its sidekick, fear (otherwise known as panic). This is completely understandable as your emotional brain is primarily designed to seek out danger of any form, either internally or externally in your environment. From an evolutionary perspective, the first task of your emotional brain is to protect you from such dangers and ensure your survival. The whole brain and body are primarily designed to fulfil this function, with everything else being a bonus.

But what happens when this essential survival apparatus turns against you? When you begin to experience acute bouts of panic or fear, or spend your life excessively anxious or catastrophising about what might occur in the future? This is the world in which countless people are living, with many finding their lives overwhelmed by anxiety. This chapter demonstrates how some simple CBT techniques can assist you to self-heal from anxiety and the emotional distress which follows in its wake.

The Difference Between Anxiety and Fear

For many people, there is no distinction between anxiety and fear – both are distressing and overwhelming. Yet, in my experience, these two emotions present separate challenges to those encountering them. A person could be anxious, for example, but rarely suffer from panic or fear. Or someone could suffer from bouts of panic or fear, or have specific phobias, but not experience any significant anxiety issues. On occasions fear and anxiety may appear together in the same person. It is important, however, to distinguish between the two emotions, as the experiences of those encountering them, and the techniques required to deal with them, differ greatly.

- *Fear* (otherwise known as panic) relates to some danger in the 'here and now' which the emotional brain regards as being a significant threat to your survival or wellbeing. It is an intensely physical experience often accompanied by a sense of dread. It is an acutely distressing emotion which has less to do with the rational brain and more to do with primitive survival mechanisms lodged in your emotional brain.

- *Anxiety*, on the other hand, relates to some danger which might occur in an imagined future, which the emotional brain regards as potentially harmful. It is therefore more to do with worrying and catastrophising as to what *might* happen in the future, rather than concerns about the immediate present. Anxiety, too, has a physical dimension, of a lower grade but more persistent variety than fear or panic. If anxiety becomes chronic or persistent, however, these physical symptoms can be equally overwhelming in nature, as with fear.

Fear and anxiety are normal emotions which all of us experience and they are, of course, appropriate and necessary in a dangerous situation. Fear would be a natural and potentially helpful emotion on encountering a mugger, for example. Or anxiety would be a natural emotion if attending a potentially life-changing job interview. Trouble begins, however, when anxiety and fear become regular intruders into your life even when there is no real underlying cause.

Which Type of Anxiety Are You Struggling With?

Countless patients begin their consultation with the statement 'I am suffering from anxiety.' For me as a doctor, this is a great beginning as they have already identified the most likely cause of their emotional distress. But when I probe further, I find most people then struggle to identify which form of anxiety they believe they are experiencing.

I have found it extremely helpful in such cases to describe the main types of anxiety that I encounter in clinical practice, and then I allow them to decide which boxes they believe they are ticking. If you find yourself suffering from anxiety, but struggling to articulate it further, then you may find the following of assistance. There are three common presenting types of anxiety:

1. Acute Anxiety – this relates to situations where you find yourself suffering from sudden bouts of acute fear or panic, with a combination of distressing sudden physical symptoms (such as heart palpations, shaking, sweating, dry mouth, muscle tension, fast shallow breathing, for example) allied to a powerful sense of dread. The commonest examples of acute anxiety are panic attacks and phobias. The primary difference between these two, as we will explore later, is that the former occurs when these distressing physical symptoms appear, seemingly out of nowhere, whilst the latter involves experiencing the same physical symptoms but assigning a place or situation as the 'reason' for their arrival.

2. Social Anxiety – this relates to a distressing condition, where those affected become both anxious and fearful about going into situations where they will have to socially interact with friends or strangers, especially in groups. Or where their anxiety is triggered by having to perform in front of others. In both situations, the person is concerned that not only will they experience the acute physical symptoms associated with fear (palpations, sweating, shallow breathing, etc.) but that others will notice these and may also note that they are blushing or awkward or uncomfortable and judge them accordingly.

3. General Anxiety – this relates to the person who is constantly emotionally anxious as they are incessantly worrying and catastrophising about what might happen in the future. They often believe that they will be unable

to cope with all of the awful things that are going to happen to them. This is often allied to a tendency to rate themselves as failures if they cannot prevent any of this happening. There are also low-grade persistent physical symptoms such as fatigue, sleep difficulties, nightmares, teeth grinding, irritable bowel and poor cognition. There is a strong link between this condition and traits such as perfectionism and behaviours such as procrastination.

If you are struggling with anxiety, you can usually quickly identify which of the forms on this list is causing your emotional distress. You may struggle with panic attacks or phobias alone and are not generally or socially anxious. You may relate solely to the world of general anxiety. You may only struggle with social anxiety. It is common, however, to find some forms intermingling. I regularly assist people with general anxiety who are also struggling with acute anxiety in the form of panic attacks or phobias. I have, on occasions, even seen all three kinds of anxiety occur in the same person, who is living consequently in a state of constant turmoil and emotional distress.

The good news for anyone who can relate to the above is that all these types of anxiety are eminently treatable, often rapidly, with some information and dedicated work using simple CBT techniques. Some of these techniques were first introduced to me by colleague and author Enda Murphy who explores them in detail in his book *5 Steps to Happiness* (visit www.SeeMe.ie). I have found that combining such CBT techniques with a basic understanding of the Neuroscience underlying anxiety and panic to be an extremely effective tool. I have seen lives completely transformed and healed by such applications. The rest of this chapter is dedicated to showing you how to achieve this objective and to demonstrate, through some clinical cases, how this would work in practice.

The Neuroscience of Anxiety

It is useful, before we begin, to briefly explore the neuroscience behind the emotions of fear and anxiety.

There are two key parts of the brain involved in anxiety and both play an important role in how you respond physically and cognitively to danger, whether real or perceived.

The first structure, which we discussed in chapter one, is the amygdala. This is the boss of your stress system, whose main function is to seek out danger, either internally in your mind or externally from your environment. When it encounters danger (real or imaginary), it kick-starts your stress system into action. If it believes the danger is acute, the amygdala triggers your adrenal stress gland (situated on top of the kidneys) to pump out bursts of the fear hormone adrenaline into your bloodstream. Adrenaline is your principal acute-stress hormone whose job it is to prepare the body to 'do a runner'. This gives rise to all the physical symptoms noted in acute anxiety (shaking, sweating, palpations, etc.).

If the amygdala believes the danger is more long-term or chronic, it triggers the release of your chronic stress hormone glucocortisol, whose job is to prepare the body for longer spells of danger. This gives rise to the chronic physical symptoms noted above, such as fatigue and poor cognition.

The second key player in the brain's response to anxiety is the prefrontal cortex (PFC). The left PFC is where we worry and ruminate. The right PFC is where we catastrophise and it has a straight hotline to the amygdala. The more we catastrophise in general anxiety, therefore, the more the amygdala encourages a steady low-grade stream of your stress hormones, especially glucocortisol and adrenaline, to be released into the body.

As a general rule, emotionally healing acute anxiety will involve challenging the amygdala alone, whilst general and social anxiety will involve challenging the PFC and to a lesser extent the amygdala.

It is useful to recognise the amygdala as being an older, less evolved organ than the more modern, intelligent PFC. I call the amygdala the 'gunslinger' as it has the capacity to fire at incredibly fast speeds if it believes that you are in significant danger. It also has a long memory for danger, so the more you avoid situations by incorrectly assigning a danger to, say, crowded spaces, the stronger it becomes. It may be helpful to think of the amygdala as more instinctive, visceral and non-verbal, as it responds to experience, and its responses are not changed by talk therapies. We can talk and reason with the PFC, however, even if some of its beliefs are quite fixed and erroneous. The good news is that CBT can teach us simple techniques to manage and reset both the amygdala and the PFC. Let's explore how this works in practice.

How to Manage Your Panic Attacks and Phobias

If you are emotionally distressed by suffering from constant panic attacks or find your life constantly disrupted by phobias, now is your opportunity to banish them, hopefully for good.

Panic Attacks

Panic attacks arise suddenly, usually without warning, and often at the most inopportune time and place. Let's take Tim, who is sitting at home, surrounded by his family and on his computer when he suddenly notices his heart pounding. He immediately assigns a 'danger' to the initial symptom which in this case is his pounding heart. The four common dangers are that he might have a heart attack, stop breathing and die; that he is going to lose control; that he is going mad, and that people around him will see him. This in turn leads to an internal demand that these symptoms must stop as they are so dangerous. This is followed quite quickly by further physical symptoms of breathing fast, stomach in knots, shaking, sweating, dry mouth and a terrible sense of dread.

The first time Tim experienced a panic attack, his partner called for an ambulance to bring him to hospital to rule out a heart attack. Although he was reassured that all was well physically, he now begins to dread this happening again. The more anxious Tim becomes about this potential danger, the more panic attacks he experiences. His GP prescribes tranquillisers and then finally antidepressants, neither of which helps. Tim learns to leave the area if a panic attack occurs and attempts to use breathing exercises, which make matters worse.

Let's write down what happened to him in an ABC format. Tim's ABC would look like this:

A – Activating Event:
- Trigger: Tim's heart begins to beat faster
- Inference/danger: I am going to have a heart attack, stop breathing, collapse or die; I am going to lose control; I am going mad; people will see me.

B – Belief/Demands:
- 'These symptoms must go away.'

C – Consequences:
- Emotional reactions: panic
- Physical reactions: stomach is in knots; shaking; sweating; heart pounding; fast breathing; dry mouth; muscles

tense; weakness and a sense of dread

- Behaviour: attends A&E via ambulance; leaves area; attends GP and trial of initially tranquillisers and then antidepressants; breathing exercises.

There will be many reading this chapter who can relate to the above story.

No matter who comes to attend me with panic attacks, their ABC will usually look like this. The chances are that the ABC of you, the reader, will be similar in nature.

If you have had a recent panic attack, go ahead and see if you can break it down as above on paper. This does two things. Firstly, it demystifies what happened to you. Secondly, it gives a clearer picture of what, up till now, may have seemed an overwhelmingly distressing occurrence.

Our next task is to assist you to understand what causes the physical symptoms laid out above in the first place. The answer is that they are caused by an adrenaline rush. This is caused by your amygdala picking up on your initial set of dangers (i.e. you are going to die) and then send information to your adrenal stress gland to pump in adrenaline, your fear hormone. Normally an adrenaline rush only lasts around eight to ten minutes in duration. But because of your safety behaviour – trying to stop the symptoms or leave the area or go to the hospital, etc, – you are telling your amygdala that you are still in danger, so it continues to encourage further adrenaline bursts and the panic attack can last up to an hour. Interestingly, the very first physical symptom (in this case, Tom's heart going faster) is the trigger for the initial panic attack, and usually caused by being stressed or excited. So in a panic attack, somewhat ironically, you are panicking about being anxious.

You may notice that I haven't once mentioned the rational brain in this discussion. This is critical as it doesn't get a look-in during this process, as the amygdala shuts it down to deal with what it sees – erroneously – as an emergency.

To banish panic attacks, it is necessary for you to take the following three steps.

1. The first step is to rationally examine these physical symptoms and decide if they are in truth dangerous at all. Many are shocked when, as a doctor, I reassure them that there is zero chance that an adrenaline rush is going to cause them any physical harm, irrespective of how often such panic attacks occur.

   This is because it is the job of your stress system to keep you safe, not harm you. You will never lose control as your amygdala will not allow this to occur. There is no link between adrenaline rushes and madness and people will rarely notice that you are experiencing such symptoms unless you hang a sign around your neck telling them. The real difficulty with these physical symptoms is that they are uncomfortable and none of us like discomfort.

2. The second step is to realize that a normal adrenaline rush will only last eight to ten minutes – if you do nothing about it. If we try to apply any safety behaviours such as racing to the hospital or taking drugs, we risk prolonging the attack. Do not leave the area. Cease trying to stop the symptoms or use breathing exercises. I can visualize many of you already 'panicking' at the thought of such behaviours. The reason for stopping them is because these physical symptoms are, in practice, completely benign in nature and therefore such behaviours are unnecessary and prolong the episode.

3. The third step is to learn to use the technique of 'Flooding'. This is where you visualize, whilst in the midst of an adrenaline rush (which is all that a panic attack is in practice), that you are stuck to the seat or ground and allow the uncomfortable physical symptoms to wash over you, without trying to stop or prevent them from happening. Once again, you may feel yourself panicking at this thought. The reality is that by not trying to stop the physical symptoms, but embracing them instead, the attack will be over in five to ten minutes.

There is, however, one crucial positive by-product of this technique – the amygdala changes its memory banks and dials down the thermostat. This means that subsequent episodes are shorter and less distressing, and that quite often, after several applications of Flooding, the amygdala switches off and your panic attacks cease. You have now calmed your gunslinger into silence. Of greater significance, you have a technique to use for the rest of your life, if panic attacks threaten to return again.

If you are struggling with panic attacks, then put the above steps into action. I have seen them transform the lives of many, and often quite rapidly. It does require some short-term pain but will lead to significant long-term gain.

Phobias

I have assisted countless people over the years as to how best to eliminate phobias from their lives and you can do the same by following the techniques shown. Phobias can cause significant emotional distress. If we take the earlier example where Mary has a phobia about going into a lift – whenever she approaches a lift, she begins to develop many of the acute physical symptoms noted above when dealing with panic attacks. She finds herself sweating, shaking, stomach in knots, heart pounding, shallow breathing, dizzy, with and an overwhelming sense of dread. Her emotion is fear or panic.

Unfortunately for poor Mary, this is only one of multiple different phobias, as she has the same reactions on entering a shopping centre, crowd or church, driving on the motorway or attempting to get on a plane or bus. Her life is slowly descending into a nightmare of fear and avoidance. What Mary is finding out the hard way is that phobias have a tendency to multiply if they are left untreated. This occurs because she learns to assign the same danger (namely that she will develop the same physical symptoms) to an increasing number of situations where she feels trapped for any reason.

Mary is not sure about why she is so afraid of going into the lift. All she knows is that she is certain something terrible will happen if she enters. She has not yet recognised what she is really afraid of: that when she goes into the lift, she will experience the acute physical symptoms of a panic attack. And that when these symptoms do arrive, she will develop one or more of the dangers she fears. Mary's major perceived danger is that she will lose control and do something terrible and that people may witness her in that state. She is also afraid that she might stop breathing due to her distress and collapse in the lift.

Understanding this fear is key as it demonstrates that it is not the situation that is the problem, but how she will physically react to being exposed to it.

Mary then begins to demand that she must not be exposed to the lift (or indeed any situation) where she develops these distressing physical symptoms. Her natural behaviour is then to avoid the lift and indeed all the other situations above, which is restricting and distressing.

Mary's ABC, written down in her own handwriting, might look like this.

A – Activating Event:
- Trigger: getting into a lift
- Inference/danger: I am going to become physically extremely anxious; I might collapse or struggle to breathe; I might die; I might lose control and go crazy; others might see me if this happens.

B – Belief/Demands:
- 'I must not be exposed to any situation (e.g. lift) where I become extremely physically anxious.'

C – Consequences:
- Emotional reactions: panic
- Physical reactions: stomach is in knots; shaking; sweating; heart pounding; fast breathing; dry mouth; muscles tense and a sense of dread
- Behaviour: avoid lifts.

I find that, no matter who comes to see me with a phobia, their ABC will look like this. The chances are high that your ABC will be similar in nature if you suffer from phobias – try it and see. The great advantage that Mary now has from this exercise is that she has a clear picture of what it is about getting into a lift that is causing her to become so distressed. She can now apply the same ABC to all her phobias.

The management of phobias is similar in practice to dealing with panic attacks but with a greater emphasis on behaviour. If you are prepared to put some hard work in, I have found that most phobias can be eliminated within three months.

Your first task is to recognise that the physical symptoms are caused, as with panic attacks, by an adrenaline rush, triggered by your amygdala sensing danger. The 'danger' in the case of most phobias is that if exposed to specific situations such as the lift, you will become physically anxious. If this happens, you might collapse, stop breathing or die; lose control and run amok; will go mad or people will see you. In my experience, the commonest dangers in phobias relate to losing control and people seeing us in that uncontrolled state. You then demand that you must not be exposed to any situation which might create this risk. The natural behaviour is to avoid. But this latter strengthens the amygdala's memory banks, confirming that there is indeed something to be afraid of, and leading us to be increasingly panicky the next time we are exposed to the situation – in Mary's case, the lift.

To banish phobias, it is necessary for you to understand what is going on, and then take the appropriate steps.

1. Remind yourself that it is not the situation (i.e. lift, crowds, planes, buses, etc.) which is the issue, but that you fear becoming physically anxious when exposed to it. The physical symptoms in turn are due to an adrenaline rush triggered by your amygdala, due to you applying a 'danger' label to the situation, i.e. the lift.

2. The physical symptoms as already discussed are not dangerous. You will not lose control, or stop breathing or collapse, people will not see you and you are not going mad. It is the job of your amygdala to keep you safe not harm you. But these physical symptoms can be extremely uncomfortable.

3. As with panic attacks, you must never try to stop these physical symptoms but instead use the Flooding technique already discussed. The more you expose yourself to what you are afraid of, and use Flooding, the faster the amygdala changes its memory until eventually it ceases firing and you can encounter the situation without fear.

4. You must therefore expose yourself repeatedly, to every single situation that you are afraid of, accept that you will become physically anxious and use Flooding to manage the resulting physical symptoms. Exposure plus Flooding will involve significant initial discomfort but under no circumstances use avoidant behaviour or safety behaviour such as taking someone with you whilst doing this exercise, as it suggests to your amygdala that you are still assigning a danger to the situation, and so perpetuating the phobia in question. In both situations the amygdala's memory for danger is otherwise increased rather than lessened. By directly challenging the situation on your own and using Flooding, you are encouraging the amygdala's memory to banish the danger for good.

Within three months of taking these steps, Mary was completely cleared of all her phobias and now understands what to do if any of them attempts to reappear. She is fully emotionally healed from her phobias, and you can be too.

How to Manage Your Social Anxiety

It is difficult for those of us who do not struggle in social situations to comprehend the levels of emotional distress generated by social anxiety – especially social interactional anxiety, which we are now going to explore. The definition of social anxiety is a state in which a person becomes extremely anxious if they have to engage in routine social interactions with friends or strangers.

Nick is twenty-five and has always struggled with social anxiety. It began in his mid-teens when a teacher mocked him publicly in front of his classmates, who subsequently ridiculed him on social media. His confidence was shattered. He is now about to attend a party for a work colleague in a busy hotel and, as always, finds himself becoming increasingly acutely physically anxious, with shaking, sweating, a dry mouth and his stomach in knots, allied to a sense of dread.

What Nick is anxious about is that when he arrives at the party, those present, especially the girls, will notice that he is anxious by spotting that he is awkward, shaking, sweating and blushing furiously. They will see him standing on his own and will also notice that he is struggling to hold down a conversation. As a result, they will judge him as being 'weird' or 'weak' or worst of all 'boring' and will shun him.

Over time, Nick has learned some avoidant and safety behaviours which are now causing him as much distress as the event itself. If possible, he avoids parties but if he cannot, as in this case, the nightmare begins. It starts at home an hour before the party with the dreaded rehearsal, where he practises in front of the mirror as to how he should present himself and rehearses in his head some 'interesting things' to say.

When he arrives at the party, he heads straight for the bar to get a few pints into him to calm his anxiety, then stays at the edge of the group, carefully avoiding starting any conversations but also trying not to appear as if separated from the others. If he is pulled into a conversation, he rehearses in his head what he will say (worrying 'will they think I am stupid?'), monitors their faces to see how he is 'going down' and leaves early to go home for the dreaded post-mortem, where he mercilessly castigates himself for making such a fool of himself and is ashamed at the prospect of having to see his colleagues the following day.

I am sure that there are many reading this who can relate to the nightmare scenario that each social occasion, even something as minor as chatting to colleagues in the café at work, presents for Nick.

Nick's ABC, written down in his own handwriting, might look like this.

A – Activating Event:
- Trigger: going to a party to meet work colleagues
- Inference/danger: whilst at the party, I will become acutely physically anxious; people will see that I am anxious as they will notice that I am awkward, sweating, blushing and that I am poor at conversation; they will then judge me as weird, weak or boring; they might then shun me.

B – Belief/Demands:
- 'I must not be exposed to any situation where people will see that I am physically anxious.' 'People will judge me negatively, and I must accept their judgement.'

C – Consequences:
- Emotional reactions: anxiety and shame
- Physical reactions: stomach is in knots, shaking, sweating, heart pounding, fast breathing, dry mouth, muscles tense, blushing and a sense of dread
- Behaviour: avoid the party if possible; rehearses at home in front of mirror, including conversation topics; on arrival goes to bar for pints; stays at edge of group;

does not initiate conversations; monitors faces; if has to speak, rehearses first in his head what he will say; leaves party early; home to face the post-mortem.

Now Nick can see, from putting down what happens in this written form, why he is becoming so distressed socially. The good news for readers who can relate to his story is that the above ABC is almost universal for every case of social anxiety I deal with.

You are not on your own when it comes to social anxiety, as up to 5 per cent of the population struggle with this condition. You may have noted already some similarities between Mary's phobias and Nick's social anxiety. In both cases they are experiencing the acute physical symptoms of fear. The difference lies in their danger. In Mary's case, she is afraid of the physical symptoms themselves. In Nick's case, his danger relates more to the assumption that others will see these physical symptoms and judge him accordingly. In practice, Nick's main issues relate to his belief that others will see that he is physically anxious and will mock his lack of skill in the art of conversation.

If you are going to deal with your social anxiety, you need to understand three important concepts, which are the key to banishing it for life. The first is that social anxiety is about perception versus reality. The second is that people are in general more concerned with themselves than others and as a consequence notice much less about us than we expect. The third is the importance of developing unconditional self-acceptance, where we cease to rate ourselves as human beings or allow others to rate us. Let's explore these three concepts in greater detail.

If you suffer from social anxiety, in general you have a perception that other people can see the physical signs of anxiety and that when you enter a social group it is as if you have a high-vis jacket on. Everyone will turn their full attention on you and begin judging you. The reality is that it is almost impossible to see the physical signs of anxiety in others, and people in social occasions are not only uninterested in assessing whether you are anxious or not, but often are unaware of your presence at all. They are fully engaged in something much more interesting, namely their own interests and agendas. This is because people are mostly concerned with what is relevant to them, and not particularly observant about things that aren't. Someone like Nick is unwittingly placing himself right at the centre of the situation by assuming that everyone will be looking at him and judging him. The truth is that everyone at that party is at the centre of their own world, and his anxiety will largely go unnoticed. It can be an enormous relief to understand this.

You will also have to practise unconditional self-acceptance, which we will be exploring later in greater detail when discussing depression and shame. In a nutshell, this will involve you having to accept that none of us can be measured, rated or judged as human beings as we are all unique and special individuals. We must understand and accept that the only part of us that can be rated is our behaviour. When we truly accept ourselves, we do not feel obliged to accept other people's' rating or judgements of us in social situations, or any other situation in life. The only behaviour that others may be entitled to rate or assess in social interactional situations are our social skills.

There will be many readers who will argue that people *can* see the physical symptoms of anxiety and that people are indeed silently assessing and judging them. In other words, they believe that their perceptions are correct and that my assertion that they are false is incorrect. To get around these false beliefs or perceptions, I suggest that you perform the following two exercises.

1. The Anxiety Inspector Exercise – for a four-week period, you must move around in any social situation you find yourself in and find the anxious people. If you truly believe these signs are unmissable, it should be easy to see who suffers from social anxiety. What will happen in practice is that you will struggle to find them at all. This is even though a significant number of those present may be socially anxious. The corollary, of course, is – if you cannot find them, then how can others find you?

2. The Supermarket Exercise – three times a week for four weeks, go to a busy supermarket, take the biggest trolley you can find, put a single item (such as a cauliflower) in it and walk around the shop for five minutes. Then find the busiest queue, and finally pay for the item in small loose change. I have seen this exercise make grown men and women blanch in terror. Their perception is that everyone will notice them and think they are 'weird'. The reality, of course, is that nobody sees or cares. Try it and see.

If you wish to eliminate social anxiety in three months, I encourage you to adopt the following behaviours:

1. Learn that the physical signs of anxiety are impossible to see, and that others are unlikely to notice them in you. To reinforce this, perform the above two exercises for a four-week period.

2. Cease all avoidant and safety behaviours, and understand that instead of protecting you they are keeping you from moving forwards with your life.

3. If you are struggling with conversation in social situations,

remember that everyone likes to talk about themselves. Try to use this insight and, instead of worrying about what you will say, get others talking about their hobbies, jobs, family, place of origin and so on. It is essential that you show genuine interest in their replies, especially via your non-verbal cues. They will then think that you are so interesting to talk to! Practise this exercise constantly for three months and you will have this skill for life. This is because the more you show genuine interest in other people, the more interesting they will find you to be. Try it and find out for yourself.

4. Learn to have a sense of humour about yourself and life. You will know your social anxiety is diminishing when you begin to realize that none of us are as important as we think we are.

How to Manage Your General Anxiety

It is my experience that for most people with symptoms of acute and social anxiety, the techniques above will either eliminate them completely or, at the least, significantly reduce them within three months.

Patients who suffer from general anxiety are constantly filled with a sense of foreboding – they assign a danger to many life situations, when no danger is present. The majority who come to me for assistance have often struggled with general anxiety from adolescence, which means many of their negative thinking and behavioural patterns have become fixed and set over time. It is often the associated physical symptoms such as fatigue and sleep difficulties which encourage them to seek out assistance. The longer we persist with unhealthy thinking and behavioural patterns, the more difficult it can be to shift them. Despite this, I have found that within six months of starting to practise CBT and with a bit of effort, you can turn these beliefs around and achieve emotional healing from the distress that often follows in the wake of these behaviours.

With general anxiety, we develop fixed irrational beliefs (discussed in chapter one) which are triggered on every occasion when something negative occurs. These beliefs persuade us to assign some danger to the triggering negative occurrence, and cause us to become emotionally anxious, with secondary physical symptoms such as fatigue and sleep difficulties, all of which lead to a plethora of unhealthy avoidant and safety behaviours. Since life is full of negative occurrences, it comes as little surprise that our irrational beliefs are constantly triggered into action.

Let's see how this would work out in practice with a patient, Susan.

Susan has suffered from general anxiety since childhood and as the years have progressed, she has found the condition increasingly paralysing. She struggles with bouts of fatigue, sleep difficulties and nightmares and persistent tension headaches. Susan worries about everything and spends her life catastrophising. It is an exhausting process that is gradually wearing her down. Her constant catastrophising is triggering her right prefrontal cortex to stimulate her amygdala, which in turn is encouraging her stress system to pump out low-grade bursts of adrenaline and especially glucocortisol, both of which are contributing to her physical symptoms.

Susan gets a call from her partner, Tom, to say that a close work colleague has been suddenly taken to hospital with a suspected heart attack. This is the trigger for Susan to become intensely anxious.

For the next few hours her mind goes into overdrive. What if

Tom is next? He has been working very hard for the previous few months on a major project. Maybe Tom is going to have a heart attack too. She can already visualize him in the hospital bed with all the machines and drips attached. It gets worse. As the day goes on, she begins to imagine the worst. Maybe Tom is going to die. How would she cope without him? And as for the children, they would be devastated. She begins to worry about how she would cope financially.

Becoming increasingly anxious, she begins to check her major source of reliable information – namely Dr Google. The more she reads medically, the more anxious she becomes as all the information seems to support her worst fears. Between her medical and financial worries, Susan's anxiety grows exponentially.

She rings her mum and then a close friend to seek reassurance, but nothing they say can convince her to stop worrying. She vows that when Tom comes home, she will convince him to attend their GP for a full check-up, perhaps even have an angiogram, which Dr Google seemed to be recommending. She begins to hit the wine bottle to calm down her anxiety levels.

When Tom returns home to let her know that his friend has indeed suffered a major heart attack, Susan's anxiety goes through the roof, especially when Tom laughs at the idea of going for a check-up, insisting that there is no history of heart disease in his family. That night, Susan suffers a restless night with terrible nightmares about Tom dying. She wakes up with her jaws aching from clenching her teeth.

She loses her appetite, has persistent tension headaches and is even more fatigued than usual. Eventually, to alleviate her anxiety, Tom agrees to go for a check-up and gets the all clear. Susan's anxiety levels fall, but still she remains on high alert. After all, he didn't have a full angiogram – could she be sure that he did not have some underlying heart disease? She would feel so bad about herself if something like this did happen.

Underlying Susan's anxiety in this case is an irrational belief that she must ensure Tom does not die prematurely from a heart attack or indeed from any cause and that if this happened she would be a failure for letting it happen.

Once again, I am sure that there are many readers who can relate to Susan's story even if the trigger for their own bout of anxiety might have been different.

Susan's ABC, written down, might look like this:

A – Activating Event:
- Trigger: phone call from partner Tom that a work colleague has been admitted to hospital with suspected heart attack
- Inference/danger: maybe Tom is next and that he too might suffer a heart attack; I can visualize him in hospital with drips and machines attached; maybe he might die; I would struggle financially and with the children; I would be a failure if this happens.

B – Belief/Demands:
- 'Tom must not die prematurely of a heart attack (or any other cause). If he does, I am a failure for letting it happen.'

C – Consequences:
- Emotional reactions: anxiety
- Physical reactions: fatigue, sleep difficulties, nightmares, teeth grinding and tension headaches
- Behaviour: worries and catastrophises; checks Dr Google; drinks some wine; rings mum and friend for reassurance; insists Tom attends GP for check-up.

Now Susan has a clear picture of what is making her so anxious. I would encourage you, if you are suffering from this condition, to do the same. There will be a great degree of repetition, as many of the ABCs for sufferers of general anxiety will be the same, if differing slightly in the information or trigger. At the heart of Susan's difficulties lie her irrational beliefs and demands. It is the 'must' that is driving her anxiety, allied to the irrational belief that she could be a 'failure' as a human being. For the word 'must' implies a totally uncompromising demand, which in life is generally impossible to fulfil.

For Susan to learn to manage her general anxiety, she needs to replace this absolute demand with the rational belief 'Of course I would prefer if Tom did not die prematurely of a heart attack or any other illness, but this is out of my control'.

The reality is that it is this demand for absolute control that is ruling her life and indeed the lives of any readers with this condition. When we demand absolute control, we are usually looking for one or more of the following: 100 per cent certainty, order, security or perfection, none of which are achievable in this life. I am sure that quite a few of you can relate to these absolute demands and recognise that you try to make them of yourself.

The good news is that it is the same demand for control that underlies all general anxiety, irrespective of the trigger. This means that if I can learn techniques to challenge this demand, I can retrain my emotional brain to become less anxious. Aside from challenging her demand for control, Susan will also have to challenge her tendency to catastrophise, cease rating herself as a failure and challenge her unhealthy behaviours.

To summarise, anxiety is a situation where we make some

impossible demands on ourselves, catastrophise how awful it will be if these demands are not met and rate ourselves as a failure if we fail to achieve these demands. It is not hard to see how difficult it would be in real life to keep going, were my world reduced to trying to satisfy the above.

To help you manage your general anxiety, I recommend that you do the following:

1. Start by challenging many of the unhelpful behaviours so prevalent in general anxiety. Avoid Dr Google like the plague: it is full of nonsensical medical and other data and will just increase your anxiety levels. Eat properly, even if you are not hungry. Be aware that we tend to search the environment around us only for evidence that our irrational beliefs and demands are true, so try to avoid falling into this trap. Cease seeking constant reassurance. Avoid alcohol and other substances as a means of controlling your anxiety levels, as they increase the risks of developing secondary addictions.

2. Never try to stop the low-grade physical symptoms, such as muscle tension, stomach in knots or sighing constantly, so common in general anxiety. Instead, learn to treat them as 'background noise' and focus on trying to change your thinking and behaviour.

3. To challenge your demand for control, I suggest the following exercise, known as the Coin Exercise. Make a list of activities that you enjoy doing on a daily or weekly basis. This could include walking, watching a series on Netflix, reading, cooking, yoga, golf, going out with your partner for meals, etc.

   For a four-week period, you will choose which activity

you do, or do not do, by the toss of a coin. Heads means yes and tails no. So if, for example, you are watching a series on Netflix, you must toss a coin before starting each episode. Heads: you can watch it, and tails: you miss it. You and your partner are going out for the night, both get ready and then toss the coin. Heads: you can go. Tails: you must cancel the night out. Ouch! And so on, till you have gone through every item on the list.

If you can let go of your need for control, and embrace a bit of uncertainty in your everyday routines, it becomes easier to accept it in bigger matters.

4. To challenge your demand for 100 per cent order, try this exercise. Ask your partner to mess up some room in your house that you like tidy and allow yourself to live with the mess for twenty-four hours. No tidying! For some people, this exercise is even more distressing than the Coin Exercise.

5. To challenge your tendency to catastrophise, try the Spilt Milk Exercise. Suppose I asked you to visualise what a glass of spilt milk would look like. If you are a catastrophist, you may visualise a large pool or puddle of milk on the table or floor – a real mess. In practice, however, only a tiny amount or a drop of milk may have been spilt. When we examine our spiralling beliefs, we quickly realize that most of our catastrophising has no basis in fact. Carry a notebook for three months and write down when you find yourself catastrophising about something, and then later, on paper, challenge your catastrophic conclusions. Bit by bit, by performing this exercise, our rational brain begins to overrule our emotional brain and we find our anxiety reducing.

6. Finally, practise the Unconditional Self-Acceptance Exercise, which we will be discussing further in the next chapter, for a period of three months.

If you persevere with the above approaches and exercises, you will find yourself gradually becoming less anxious and more accepting of life with all its foibles and uncertainties. This in turn will lead to a reduction in the physical symptoms which can be so debilitating.

Let's now turn our attention to one of the most distressing human emotions of all, namely depression.

3. Depression

Most of us have experienced having 'the blues' or have been through periods of time where our mood is flat or down. You may be someone who has experienced longer spells of depressed mood as a result of bouts of clinical depression. Sometimes you may be unsure as to which of these two scenarios apply in your case: am I just feeling the blues or am I genuinely clinically depressed? If you can relate to some or all of the above, read on as we explore how emotional healing in both situations may be just around the corner.

For decades, there has been considerable confusion in the eyes of public, professionals and media commentators alike between the emotion of depression (with a little 'd') and Depression (with a big 'D') the clinical illness. This confusion has caused significant difficulties for patients, especially those struggling with serious depression. Both conditions can cause significant emotional distress. Hopefully, by the end of this chapter, if you are struggling with either you will be able to manage them better. We begin by exploring depression the emotion and then later will contrast it with Depression the illness.

Depression the Emotion

Most of us can relate to this emotion. It is often described as 'feeling down' or 'going through a bout of the blues'. If it persists, it can be described as a bout of low mood, which can be present for days or even up to a week or two and then lifts. It can be triggered by many negative life experiences. There is little doubt that some of us have a tendency to experience this emotion more regularly and possibly more intensely than others. We are all aware of friends, loved ones or colleagues who constantly look at the gloomier side of life, perhaps those for whom life has been harsh, with loss or disappointments, illness or other negative experiences shaping their view of the world.

There can be little doubt also that some of us are by personality sunny and optimistic and others less so. Young people who have been bullied by peers or have grown up in hypercritical homes or other negative environments are especially at risk of depression. Negative experiences as adults, such as workplace bullying, can also create the environment for this emotion to flourish. Those who suffer from Impostor Syndrome, often women, regularly struggle with this emotion as they believe that they are 'not good enough' or will be caught out as 'a fraud'. Finally, those of us who are exposed to the raw emotions of grief at any point in our lives may encounter this emotion as well. We will be exploring grief in detail later in the book.

Depression the emotion is one of the most important unhealthy negative emotions. We classify it as an unhealthy negative emotion as it makes us feel bad about ourselves and is often associated with unhealthy resultant behaviours such as isolating ourselves from others. This emotion is frequently triggered by persistent negative internal personal self-ratings, which we will be discussing later. It is these self-critical irrational beliefs that drive the emotion. There is a strong body of opinion that believes that such underlying irrational beliefs are often 'wired' into the emotional brain during childhood, adolescence and young adult life.

Your brain is wired in such a manner that the rational brain is usually able to keep the emotional brain (in the form of the amygdala) in check, so most of us, whilst feeling emotionally depressed for short periods, will tend to come out of such periods naturally. Your mood lifts, the clouds scatter and rays of sunshine enter your life again, usually within a week or ten days.

It is my experience over countless consultations that depression the emotion is regularly associated with other unhealthy negative emotions such as hurt, guilt, anxiety and shame. This makes sense as some of these are 'rating-driven' emotions, i.e. they are initiated by some stated or implied negative self-judgements or rating of ourselves as human beings.

Because all of us can relate so easily to this emotion, the assumption is that everyone who is suffering from any form of low mood should be able to 'snap out of it' and somehow regain their normal mood. But as we will discover later, those who are clinically depressed may not find this easy to achieve.

If you can relate to this emotion and find that it is triggered easily by negative life experiences, it is essential to learn techniques to manage your emotions. Otherwise your life may become hard to enjoy, even though you are not clinically depressed. Let's explore this further.

How to Manage the Emotion of Depression

If you are experiencing this emotion on a regular basis, it is likely that you have developed fixed irrational beliefs about yourself, which were triggered by negative life situations. Such beliefs, as previously explored, are usually created in your formative years. The emotion of depression can be accompanied by physical symptoms in the form of low-grade fatigue, sleep difficulties or a loss of appetite or interest in life lasting for several days. It may also be associated with some social withdrawal or avoidance, a tendency to isolation and varying degrees of internal self-criticism during such periods. Since our busy lives are full of negative occurrences, it comes as little surprise that such irrational beliefs are being constantly triggered into action. To manage these irrational beliefs and unhelpful behaviours, I have found the usage of CBT techniques to be especially useful.

Let's meet Megan, who learns, with the assistance of Dr Jim, how to apply such techniques.

Megan's Story

At twenty-seven, Megan is referred by her family doctor to see Dr Jim, having become emotionally distressed following the break-up of her five-year relationship. Her GP did not believe that she was clinically depressed but felt that she did require some CBT assistance to deal with this life-adjustment issue.

Megan came from a hypercritical family where she was put down regularly by both parents, especially her father, often over minor issues. By adulthood, she tended to be hard on herself and extremely self-critical. She had regular periods of low mood, usually of short duration, but would become quite withdrawn and quiet during such periods. She believed that it was this pattern of behaviour that had led her partner Dave to finally leave her, as she felt he struggled to cope with her 'moods'. She also shared with Dr Jim about her difficult upbringing and her negative view of herself. She suffered from Impostor Syndrome at work and had, in her words, low self-esteem.

Dr Jim listens empathetically to Megan's story and offers to assist her to manage such issues by using some CBT techniques. He explains about rational and irrational beliefs and lays out the ABC concepts, explaining how they will employ this system to locate and manage her irrational beliefs. They decide to use Dave's breaking off the relationship as the trigger.

'And how did this make you feel emotionally?' asks Dr Jim.

'I felt quite depressed for at least a week,' she replies, 'and then found myself alternating between being anxious and depressed. It's been like that ever since he left.'

'What was your behavioural response to these emotions?' asks Dr Jim. 'In other words, what did you do when you felt like this?'

'I found myself becoming increasingly socially withdrawn,' Megan replies. 'I kept going over in my head everything which happened, especially at night.'

She also admits to catastrophising about her future, eating poorly, drinking more wine than usual and, with a red face, to checking out Dave's social media to see what he was doing.

'And how did these emotions make you feel physically?' asks Dr Jim.

'I felt tired and struggled with motivation and concentration,' Megan replies.

They decide to add this information to Megan's ABC:

A – Activating Event:
- Trigger: Dave, her long-term partner, breaks off their relationship
- Inference/danger:

B – Belief/Demands:

C – Consequences:

- Emotional reactions: depression and anxiety
- Physical reactions: fatigue, poor concentration, sleep difficulties, poor motivation
- Behaviour: withdrawing socially, ruminating, catastrophising about the future, drinking excessively, eating poorly, checking ex-partner's social-media sites.

Dr Jim then begins to explore what inferences Megan had taken from the break-up of her relationship that led her to experience her emotions of depression and anxiety.

He begins by asking Megan, 'What was it about Dave leaving you that caused you to feel depressed?'

'I felt that he was right to leave me,' she replies sadly. 'It only confirmed what I have always thought about myself, that I am an uninteresting, useless, boring person to be around. I also felt like such a failure, being unable to hold on to such a special person.'

'Anything else?' asks Dr Jim.

Megan looks away and tears appear, 'It confirmed what I have always believed about myself – that I am worthless!'

After a moment of silence, Dr Jim asks, 'What was it about him leaving you that caused you to feel anxious?'

'I began to worry that I would be left on my own,' Megan replies. 'That I would never meet someone like Dave again. I could visualise myself alone and lonely going into my later years.'

'So now let's examine what irrational beliefs were triggered by Dave's departure and the inferences you assigned to them,' says Dr Jim.

With Dr Jim's assistance and after some detailed discussions, Megan decides that her belief in relation to her emotion of depression was that because Dave had left her, she was 'useless, a failure, boring and worthless'. They also agree that her irrational belief in relation to her emotion of anxiety took the form of a demand that 'she must not finish up alone and lonely, and that if this happens, that she would be a failure'.

They add this information to complete Megan's ABC:

A – Activating Event:
- Trigger: Dave, her long-term partner, breaks off their relationship
- Inference/danger: that he was right to leave me; it confirmed what I have always believed about myself – that I am useless, boring, a failure and worthless; I might be left on my own for life; I might finish up alone and lonely.

B – Belief/Demands:
- 'Because Dave left me, I am useless, boring, worthless and a failure.' 'I must not finish up alone and lonely. If I do, I am a failure.'

C – Consequences:
- Emotional reactions: depression and anxiety
- Physical reactions: fatigue, poor concentration, sleep difficulties, poor motivation
- Behaviour: withdrawing socially, ruminating, catastrophising about the future, drinking excessively, eating poorly, checking ex-partner's social-media sites.

Megan now has a clearer understanding of why she has become so emotionally distressed following her break-up.

Dr Jim then explains that there is little point in trying to challenge her emotions.

'That is just the way we feel about something, and trying to feel differently is a pointless exercise. However, we can learn a lot by exploring and challenging your unhealthy thinking and behavioural patterns.'

They begin by Dr Jim challenging Megan's behaviours and asking whether they were in any way assisting her in relation to her situation. She agrees that withdrawing socially, drinking more, eating poorly and checking her ex's social media had only worsened her situation, as had her tendency to ruminate and catastrophise. They discuss healthier alternatives. They agree that reducing her alcohol intake, improving her nutrition and ceasing to check her ex's social media would be better for her mental and physical health than her current behaviours.

The real work begins, however, when Dr Jim starts to challenge Megan's irrational beliefs and demands. He is especially interested in her belief that she was 'useless, a failure, boring and worthless'.

'Is this a rational or irrational belief?' he asks.

Megan replies that she has always believed this about herself, so assumed it was rational.

This leads to a long discussion on whether a human being can be rated or described in such a manner. He asks her to perform a Rating Exercise where she has to rate herself as a person between one and a hundred on a scale written down on paper, with a hundred suggesting she was incredible and one that she was crap. Megan finds this difficult to do, but eventually marks herself in on the scale at thirty.

'And where do you believe others rate you?' asks Dr Jim.

Megan marks herself at forty.

'And when Dave left you,' asks Dr Jim, 'where would you have marked yourself in then?'

Megan marks herself down to five. She also marks herself down at thirty when asked how others would view her if hearing this news.

'But can a human being be rated in such a manner at all?' asks Dr Jim. He then admits that the exercise was a trap that Megan and so many others fall into.

'Human beings are too special, wonderful and unique,' he continues 'to be boxed in and measured like commodities in this manner.'

Following an intense discussion, they agree that the only part of a human being which can be rated in practice is their behaviour or skills and talents.

For Megan, this was a mind-blowing conversation.

'But why have I spent my whole life believing that I can be rated or judged in this manner?' she asks.

This leads to a discussion on how all of us have an internal critic, which Dr Jim calls the 'pathological critic'.

'This is the voice in your head, which is so self-critical of everything we say and do,' he explains. 'It is the voice which makes you believe that you are worthless, or useless, or boring or a failure, for example.'

Megan can relate to this voice as it had been a lifelong companion. Dr Jim explains how our childhood and adolescent experiences can inform this negative, internally self-destructive bully and turn it into a monster. Megan recounts how her father had always been hypercritical of her, and wonders if this could have been the source of her current difficulties and the origin of the critical voice in her head? Dr Jim agrees that growing up in such an environment would indeed explain why this voice was playing such an important role in her view of herself.

He then introduces her to the world of Unconditional Self-Acceptance, where she learns to become comfortable in her own skin by accepting herself as the special, unique human being that she is. To achieve this, she has to cease rating or judging herself, or allowing others to do so, but would be free to rate and take responsibility for her behaviour.

'What a wonderful place that would be to inhabit,' Megan says, with tears in her eyes. 'I only wish that I could be comfortable in my own skin.'

Dr Jim then gives her the Unconditional Self-Acceptance Exercise to perform for the following three months. She must carry a notebook for three months, and any time she finds herself rating herself as a failure or useless or worthless, etc., she must write in the trigger and her rating from one to one hundred. Then later, on paper, she is to challenge her rating as follows:

- Can a human being be described as useful or useless?
- Is this rating more a description of your behaviour, skills or talents?

Megan begins to understand that she has been defining herself in vague, self-critical statements, but on closer analysis these statements are false.

Dr Jim agrees, 'Your pathological critic is trying to convince you that you are useless as a person, but human beings cannot be divided into two groups, one useful and the other not. You can certainly analyse your behaviour in the form of your skills or talents as being useful or useless. You might be a useful business executive but a useless cook, for example. Neither of these will define who you are as a human being, however.'

They proceed to challenge the other terms which her pathological critic had used to beat Megan up with. She was not 'worthless' or 'weak' or 'boring' or 'a failure', etc., as all of these were simply false negative beliefs about herself. Megan was most taken by the realization that she could not be regarded as 'a failure' as a person but could only fail at a task at a moment in time, and that the only failure in life was not getting back up again and having another go.

What Megan began to understand was that she had to separate who she was as a person from her behaviour and skills.

'It is as if I have a separate core,' she suggests, 'and that is inviolate. But surrounding this core are all the other facets of me as a person in the guise of my skills and talents and behaviours.'

Dr Jim agrees. 'By challenging your bullying pathological critic in this manner, on paper, your rational brain gradually begins to '"shut down"' the bully in your emotional brain as you increasingly find yourself challenging these negative, self-critical, personal barbs. You begin to realise these self-critical thoughts are nonsense.'

Megan vows to perform this exercise diligently over the following three months.

Dr Jim then challenges her belief that 'she must not be left alone and lonely'.

'Is this rational?' he asks. Following discussion, Megan accepts that this is an impossible demand to achieve in real life, for she has no control over what would happen in the months and years to come and that there is no such thing as 100 per cent certainty in life. She accepts, however, that on the law of averages there is a reasonably good chance that she might meet someone with whom she could spend the rest of her life.

Dr Jim gives her the Coin Exercise to help her understand this concept emotionally (see page 56). They also discuss the Spilt Milk Exercise to challenge her tendency to catastrophise (see page 57).

Over the following nine months, Megan's emotional life is

transformed. She finds the Unconditional Self-Acceptance Exercise challenging at the beginning, but becomes increasingly comfortable in her own skin. She notices and accepts so many positive aspects about herself that she had previously suppressed, and even comes to like herself. Gradually but firmly, she puts her pathological critic back in its box.

She also becomes more realistic about relationships, accepting that sometimes they work and sometimes they don't, but that neither outcome defines who she is as a person. She notes how her emotion of depression is increasingly becoming a distant memory.

A year later, she reveals to Dr Jim that she has met a new partner. For the first time since she was a teenager, Megan finds herself at ease with both herself and her new relationship. Her hard work and perseverance have paid off.

Key Learning Points

There are several practical messages that you can learn from Megan's story which can assist you to manage the emotion of depression:

1. At the heart of this emotion is an irrational belief, which may have been present since your childhood or adolescence, that you can be 'rated or measured' as a human being. That you as a human being can be defined in absolute terms such as being 'useless', 'weak', 'worthless', etc., all of which are false, illogical beliefs about yourself.
2. It is your internal pathological critic, which is formed during those early years, that drives such false beliefs. When anything negative happens to us in life, the pathological critic is the source of the relentless self-critical messages that we beat ourselves up with.

3. The antidote is to develop Unconditional Self-Acceptance, where you learn to accept yourself without any conditions, neither rating yourself as a human being nor allowing others to do so; but free to challenge and take responsibility for your behaviour and skills and talents. This will result in the sense that you are comfortable in your own skin.

4. The short-cut to developing this skill is to perform the Unconditional Self-Acceptance Exercise (see page 68) for a period of three months.

Depression, the Illness

Apart from the ravages of grief, there are few other conditions in life which can damage your emotional world as much as a bout of clinical depression. It can leave you in tatters emotionally, sucking joy, peace and inner contentment out of your life, causing intense emotional distress for both you and those who care for you. The deep-seated emotional distress of depression as an illness can lead to hopelessness, helplessness and a belief that you will never emerge out of this place of despair and inner emotional pain. My message of hope is that you can also be healed from this condition, and I have seen it happen countless times.

In this section, I am going to give an insight into the world inhabited by those with depression as an illness, and to demonstrate the significant differences between depression the emotion and the ravages of Depression the illness. For the rest of this section, we are going to describe the latter as Major Depression (often described by professionals as Major Depressive Disorder or MDD).

What is Major Depression?

Major Depression (or MDD) is an illness which affects up to 15 to 20 per cent of the population. It is a physical, cognitive and psychological illness which normally comes in bouts lasting anything from six to twelve months in duration. It is twice as common in women as in men. It often begins in adolescence for the first time. It is important to note that 25 per cent of all cases of major depression present with their first bout between the ages of thirteen and eighteen (occasionally earlier). Many of these bouts are both unrecognised and untreated, as the young person may not understand what is happening to them, with the bout only subsequently coming to light when a further episode arrives, often at college. A further 25 per cent will first present with a depressive episode between eighteen and twenty-five years of age. In total therefore, 50 per cent of all cases will present for the first time between thirteen and twenty-five.

Others may present later, frequently during or following pregnancy, or sometimes following a period of intense stress. There is a final cohort who may present for the first time from the age of sixty onwards, so-called 'late onset depression'.

How Does Major Depression Present?

The answer to this question is critical, as our first task is to demonstrate that Depression the illness is a completely different experience from depression the emotion. During a bout of clinical depression, you are likely to experience some or all of the following symptoms, which clearly demonstrate that this condition is affecting much more than simply your 'emotions', even if these are important players in the condition. Let's describe firstly the physical, cognitive and psychological symptoms which you may experience and then discuss what is felt 'clinically' to constitute a bout of this illness.

Physical Symptoms
These include the following:

1. Fatigue – The fatigue described by most with MDD is a deep-seated state of absolute exhaustion where even the simplest task becomes a major ordeal. It is a form of mental fatigue, but it will seem physical to you. You may stop all forms of exercise, in the mistaken belief that this will conserve whatever energy remains. Fatigue can intrude into every area of your life. You may avoid social contact, as it will mean expending energy you simply do not have. If you are a student, you may struggle to find the energy to study, or if an employee, to work. You may find dragging yourself from one end of the day to the other a constant struggle.
2. Sleep Difficulties – You may find your sleep patterns becoming literally a nightmare. Either struggling to get to sleep, experiencing broken, unrefreshed sleep, or waking up early at four or five in the morning, unable to return to sleep, just lying there, with your emotional mind running wild with ruminations.
3. Appetite Difficulties – You many find yourself at either end of the spectrum. You may lose all interest in food as you are not experiencing any enjoyment from it and lose weight rapidly. Or you may find yourself comfort-eating continuously and piling on weight.
4. Loss of Drive – You may discover that you are losing

your normal drive, enthusiasm and interest to carry out normal, routine everyday tasks. Your life can feel as if it has become an arid wasteland where nothing matters. This can lead to a loss of libido, which can cause difficulties with partners. It can also lead to a loss of interest in your hobbies, work or other projects or studies.

Cognitive Symptoms

For me, the area of clinical depression which has been most overlooked over the past fifty years or so, especially by sufferers, is that this condition really messes up important cognitive processes in the brain. These symptoms cause significant distress in the lives of those affected by MDD. Even worse, they are poorly understood by both the person suffering from the condition and those who share their domestic and working lives with them. This leads to increased emotional distress and pain. It is also one of the defining differences between the illness and the emotion, so the presence or absence of such symptoms can be useful in distinguishing one from the other.

During a bout of MDD, you may experience some of the following cognitive symptoms:

1. Poor Memory – You may notice that you are struggling with both your short- and long-term memory. This can make retaining information extremely challenging. Dates, appointments and everyday working memory can be a struggle. This may be a significant issue for you either at work, at home or academically.

2. Reduced Concentration – You may find focusing on or retaining information impossible. Simple tasks such as checking your phone or reading the paper, reading

documents at work or academically become a frustrating exercise. Many students will drop out of college during a bout of this condition. Or workers suffer from presenteeism. You may be able to relate to either.

3. Indecisiveness or Difficulties with Problem-Solving – If you notice that you are suddenly struggling to make a decision or problem-solve a task which normally you would fly through, then it is likely that your cognition is down. These so-called executive functions of the brain are essential for your normal working and domestic life.

4. Reduced Psychomotor Speed – This refers to the speed at which your body obeys your brain. If you notice that tasks seem to be taking twice as long to get through in all areas of your life, then this too is an indicator that your cognition is down.

Psychological Symptoms

These are the classical symptoms that most of us understand as 'Depression' the illness. You may notice that I have dealt with the other two groups of symptoms first. This is to demonstrate that whilst these classical symptoms are clearly important, this condition is as much a physical and cognitive illness as a psychological one.

If you are going through a bout of MDD, you will generally be experiencing some or all of the following:

1. Depressed Mood – Earlier, we discussed that while the emotion of depression is unpleasant, it is usually of short duration. In MDD, however, you will notice that this emotion is more intense and long-lasting. It is present day after day, week after week, month after month, destroying your

inner emotional reserves and threatening to overcome them. When emotions last for longer periods, we call them moods. In MDD, you may find that this depressed mood is constantly present, and often at its worst first thing in the morning, which is why you may feel like staying in bed and not facing the day.

This depressed mood can be a companion for up to nine months or more if left untreated. It is best described as like being in a dark hole or well, with high walls all around, surrounded by darkness, with only a brief glimpse of light visible. One may feel there is no way of climbing out. It is a world of deep-seated emotional pain, a shrivelling-up of your very soul. Mothers have often described it as a pain more intense than labour. Others have described days with major depression as feeling as if there is no end to the wasteland within.

2. Anhedonia – This is where you find that you are achieving no pleasure from normal human actions and interactions such as food, sex and social interaction. It is as if joy has been sucked out of the atmosphere and nothing gives you a 'buzz' any longer. You may be finding this extremely distressing.

3. Negative Thinking – You may irrationally believe that you are worthless, which, as we have explored, is the thinking behind the emotion of depression. You may also see little hope for yourself or the future. Persistent, continuous, negative thinking about yourself or the world is called rumination. This is where the thoughts go around and around your head – sometimes called the washing machine in your head.

4. Suicidal Thoughts – It may be routine, during a bout, for

you to experience some thoughts of self-harm, and this can be a relief for some to know. Whilst extremely distressing, thankfully these thoughts rarely progress into actions. However, if you have been investigating methods as to how you would take your own life, then it is essential that you seek out immediate professional assistance. Either talk to someone close to you, or ring a relevant helpline, as the presence of these thoughts indicates that your mood may be significantly dropping.

To make a clinical diagnosis of MDD usually requires the presence of either significantly reduced mood for a minimum period of two to four weeks or the presence of anhedonia for a month, combined with four or five of the other symptoms above. In practice, over decades, it is my experience that significant bouts of this illness nearly always involve most of the physical, cognitive and psychological symptoms noted above. Depending on the severity of the symptoms described, clinical depression can be assessed as mild, moderate or severe. This classification is important when it comes to management.

The Neuroscience of Depression

It is beyond the scope of this book to explore in detail exactly what is happening in the brain and body during a bout of MDD, but it is helpful to have a basic understanding of the process in order to see how it may be treated.

1. MDD is no longer perceived as being a 'chemical illness', as was believed erroneously for so long, but rather a breakdown in the neurocircuitry between the rational

and emotional brains, especially between the amygdala and prefrontal cortex. The amygdala is seen as the source of the negative emotions we encounter.

2. Most of the physical, cognitive and psychological symptoms occur secondary to this dysfunctional neurocircuitry.

3. Some of us are vulnerable to bouts of this condition, due to a combination of genetic vulnerability and environmental influences when growing and developing. If we encounter significant life stressors either during adolescence or later, this vulnerability may trigger the brain into a negative mode which attacks the neurocircuitry underlying cognition.

4. We also know that our body's stress and immune systems are significantly affected during a bout of depression. There is evidence, for example, of higher levels of our stress hormone, glucocortisol, and an increase in pro-inflammatory markers in the bloodstream. This explains the increased risk of both diabetes and heart disease in those who are struggling with this illness. Another pointer to the physical nature of this condition.

5. We don't yet understand why a bout of depression 'switches off', but it is most likely that the brain manages to regain homeostasis or 'balance' within nine to twelve months, even if no therapy is applied.

6. The persistent negative ruminations so prevalent in this condition are felt to be linked to an important circuit in the brain called the Default Mode Network (DMN) which is increasingly seen as a key player in how we introspect. This was an area that was found to 'come alive' when we cease performing specific tasks. But on further exploration it was also found to be an essential component in our

capacity to daydream and self-reflect. It contains many structures involved in our management of emotional and contextual memories. It also involves areas of both the limbic system and the prefrontal cortex. Whilst one would expect the DMN to be hyperactive in MDD, as this part of the brain is so relevant to introspection and rumination, this does not seem to be the case. Instead, there is now evidence which points to a heightened activity between the DMN and a key junction point between the emotional and logical brain, as one of the drivers of these ruminations so prevalent in depression. For those who would like to know more, see the bibliography for further reading.

The Experience of Depression

It is useful to describe how you may be feeling if in the throes of a bout of clinical depression. You may be constantly tired and struggling to get out of bed in the morning due to a combination of low mood, lack of motivation and exhaustion from lack of sleep and persistent fatigue. You may be struggling to concentrate, focus on the most basic of tasks, retain details in your working memory, make decisions or problem-solve. You may functionally be struggling with everyday tasks and chores due to a combination of the above. You may be constantly ruminating as a result, telling yourself that you really are 'useless' and not worth being around.

You may be finding yourself apathetic about everything ('just don't care') and have ceased enjoying the normal pleasures of life such as food, sex and socializing. You may be avoiding the latter, believing that you are just a burden on those with whom you would be interacting. You may find yourself increasingly anxious, frustrated and ashamed of what others might think of you. You may believe that they think of you – as you think of yourself – as 'weird' or 'abnormal'. It is likely that you believe that there is little point in considering seeking assistance, as you, in your own mind, are the problem. You may even be struggling with thoughts of self-harm and in a smaller number of cases, seriously considering removing the problem by ending your life.

How to Manage Your Bout of Depression

If you can relate to the above description, it is clear that this is not simply an experience of the emotion of depression. Rather, you are experiencing a bout of an illness which is affecting many aspects of your brain and body. When considering management of such a bout, it is important to take a holistic approach, as if the illness in question is, for example, diabetes. In the case of the latter, we do not simply use medication if required, but also advise changes to lifestyle in the areas of diet and physical exercise and some counselling as to how best to manage the condition. This is the approach which we use in relation to our management of depression.

At the heart of this approach we must put at the centre of our discussion the word 'function'. Only those who have struggled with bouts of major depression can genuinely understand the importance of this word. For them, each day is a battle to keep functioning in the different domains of life.

I am now going to briefly lay out the three strands of any holistic therapy package for treating major depression.

1. Lifestyle Changes – These include trying to exercise for thirty minutes, five times a week (in three parts daily if necessary); proper nutrition; ceasing or significantly

reducing alcohol consumption; trying to explore major stressors in your life. This might involve exploring work pressures, relationship difficulties, family problems and so on.

2. Talk Therapy – The form of talk therapy found to be of greatest assistance in the management of MDD is CBT and we will be demonstrating this in practice later. Other forms of talk therapy can include counselling and interpersonal therapy. You can learn how to apply CBT techniques further down, in John's story.

3. Drug Therapy – This has often been the controversial part of the treatment package. I see drug therapy as being of assistance in situations where your mood may be quite low and especially if you are struggling with the cognitive difficulties discussed above. In my experience, applying CBT techniques to somebody who is struggling with their cognition is almost a waste of time for both parties. This is because it is impossible for the patient to either concentrate on, or remember the work done.

Drug therapy in the form of antidepressants tries to calm down the emotional brain, especially the amygdala, which allows the rational brain to regain control and to improve physical and cognitive dysfunctions. The medications primarily target serotonin and noradrenaline systems in the brain and these have some side-effects, especially initial nausea, agitation, increased suicide ideation in those under twenty-five (these side-effects usually clear within four weeks) and sexual dysfunction, amongst others. Drug therapy should be considered as part of a package, to be used especially if cognition is an issue. They work for some patients and not for others. Medication takes two weeks to kick in and, if effective, mood and cognition will improve significantly from one month onwards. They should be taken for a period of at least six months from the time that you feel better (usually six to eight weeks) and should be withdrawn slowly at the end of this period.

There is a belief amongst mental-health professionals that the current drugs are useful, but it is also recognised that we have yet to discover a potent, side-effect-free drug that acts quickly and efficiently to allow the person to get back to normal life as soon as possible. The ideal drug would have to lift mood, improve physical symptoms and above all restore full cognition.

There is some interesting research taking place exploring whether the general anaesthetic ketamine, which acts on the prefrontal cortex itself, might be of assistance. There is also an increased interest in the use of some psychedelic substances. The most promising is an extract of the psychedelic drug LSD, called psilocybin (see bibliography) which it is believed acts by dissolving the default mode network (DMN), which allows talk therapies such as CBT to reset this network into something more positive. We will have to see if this and other research bears fruit into the future.

It is best to assess which of the above three strands are appropriate for you with the assistance of your family doctor or specialist. The secret is to be honest with yourself and this is difficult with clinical depression. *For this is the only illness in the whole of medicine which tries to convince you that 'you' are the problem.* Which means that you may not be able to see the solution by yourself.

This insight is essential when it comes to considering how to manage a bout of major depression. Remember that 'it' is the problem, not 'you'. Focus mostly on function. If you are a busy parent, a student or holding down an important job, then being able to function in these areas is essential. You may, for example, prefer to only consider lifestyle changes and talk therapy. This is fine if dealing with mild to possibly moderate bouts of depression. But if you are really struggling, especially cognitively or otherwise, then do consider discussing drug therapy with your family doctor. Despite all the negativity, I have seen these drugs revolutionize a person's life and assist them to make lifestyle changes and become involved in talk therapy, especially CBT. The latter, as explored earlier in the chapter, involves challenging the pathological critic and developing Unconditional Self-Acceptance.

Let's now visit with John, who is twenty-two and is considering dropping out of his college course, due to an undiagnosed bout of clinical depression. He attends Dr Jim, on the advice of the campus counsellor, for an assessment.

John's Story

John is a twenty-two-year-old undergraduate, whose life, halfway through his final year at college, begins to implode. It began with fatigue, followed swiftly by a sudden drop in mood, insomnia, increased levels of anxiety and difficulties with concentration and memory, which led him to rapidly fall behind in his studies, barely passing his mid-term assignments. He struggles to get out of bed in the morning, withdraws socially and breaks off his current relationship with Jill as he believes that 'she could do better'. His alcohol intake increases as he struggles to cope with how he feels. He is ashamed to let family and friends know of his difficulties and even begins to consider self-harm. Jill, increasingly concerned, convinces him to attend the college counsellor, who persuades him to attend Dr Jim for an assessment.

He reveals all to Dr Jim, who is empathetic to his situation and suggests that John has slipped into a bout of clinical depression and queries as to whether he had ever experienced these symptoms in the past. John notes that he had experienced something similar in his mid-teens, but that it had passed after four or five months. It also turned out that his mum had suffered from several bouts of post-natal depression.

This leads to a discussion on clinical depression, what it is, how it comes in bouts, how it affects us physically, cognitively and emotionally, and the importance of managing such bouts effectively to reduce incidence of further episodes in the future. John is relieved that it was not all in his mind and that there was indeed a reason for his current difficulties. He also admits that he was struggling to concentrate on or retain the content of his discussion with Dr Jim.

'It's as if my mind is in a fog,' he explains, 'which is why I was going to drop out of the course.'

Dr Jim explains that this is a common but poorly recognised symptom of this condition, 'It's as if the brain mechanisms involved in memory and concentration are working at half-speed and everything becomes a major chore.'

This leads to a discussion on the importance of 'function' when assessing the effects of clinical depression, and why it is so important to include cognition in the discussion. John admits that he had come to believe that the difficulties with his studies lay with himself, and this had made him feel worse, mood-wise.

'Try to remember from now on,' suggests Dr Jim, 'that "it" is the problem, not you.' John found this insight extremely empowering and vowed to embrace it from then on.

They then discussed the role of lifestyle changes, talk therapies such as CBT and the role of drug therapy. Dr Jim suggests that in John's case he feels that all three should form part of the solution. John is anxious about the use of anti-depressants because of the stigma surrounding them. Dr Jim agrees that they are not a panacea for all ills, but could play an important role in helping John to become 'functional' by lifting his mood, improving some of his physical symptoms and most of all his cognition, which in turn would allow John to engage in talk therapy such as CBT.

'It would be pointless to explore CBT techniques with you now, if you are unable to focus on or retain the relevant information,' he adds.

John now has a clearer understanding of how best to manage his current bout of depression. On Dr Jim's advice, he agrees to attend the college GP for assessment and possible drug treatment. John also accepts Dr Jim's suggestion that perhaps he should discuss his difficulties with his college tutor and decide whether he should take some time out on medical grounds. They also agree that when John is feeling better and has improved cognition-wise, that he would return to Dr Jim for some assistance with his thinking.

John returns six weeks later, feeling considerably better. His mood is improving, physical symptoms are diminishing and his concentration and memory are beginning to recover. The college GP had suggested some lifestyle changes, liaised with the college authorities to allow John to take some time out on medical grounds, and prescribed a course of antidepressants, which John tolerated better than expected and which had led to the above improvements. Even the thoughts of self-harm had faded.

'I am still struggling with my inner demons,' he admits. 'Even though I am feeling better in so many ways, the voices in my head are still pulling me down.'

Dr Jim then offers to assist him to deal with these demons by applying some CBT techniques and John readily agrees. He explains about rational and irrational beliefs and lays out the ABC concepts, explaining how they will employ this system to locate and manage his irrational beliefs. They decide to use John's current bout of depression as the trigger.

'And how did this make you feel emotionally?' asks Dr Jim.

'I felt both depressed and frustrated,' replies John.

'Now, what was your behavioural responses to these emotions?' asks Dr Jim. 'What did you do when you felt like this?'

John admits to withdrawing socially, spending too much time in bed, drinking too much, losing interest in food and sex, breaking off from his girlfriend Jill and considering self-harm. They also agree that his depression had given rise to the many physical and cognitive symptoms already described above.

They add this information to John's ABC:

A – Activating Event:
- Trigger: his current bout of depression
- Inference/danger:

B – Belief/Demands:

C – Consequences:
- Emotional reactions: depression and frustration
- Physical reactions: fatigue; poor concentration; difficulties with memory, sleep, appetite and motivation
- Behaviour: withdrawing socially; breaking off current relationship; ruminating; drinking excessively; eating poorly; spending too much time in bed; considering self-harm.

Dr Jim then begins to explore what inferences that John had taken from his current bout of clinical depression had led him to experience the emotions of depression and frustration.

He begins by asking John, 'What was it about this current bout of depression that caused you to feel so depressed?'

'It made me believe that I was stupid for starters,' replies John. 'Useless, of little value to anyone and a failure for not being able to snap out of it by myself. I also believed that I was abnormal or weird as "normal people" do not think and feel like this.'

'And why frustrated?' asks Dr Jim.

'Why me?' replies John. 'Everyone else around me seemed to be getting on with their lives, unlike me, who was struggling to function. Why was I the one who had to cope with the pain and distress of this condition?'

'So now let's examine what irrational beliefs were triggered by this current bout of depression and the inferences you assigned to it,' says Dr Jim. 'This usually takes the form of some absolute demands you were making about the trigger, which in this case was your current bout of depression.'

Following some discussions, John decides that his belief in relation to his bout of depression was 'that because he had "Depression" he was weird, useless, weak, a failure and worthless'. And that his belief in relation to his emotion of frustration was 'that he should not have to put up with the discomfort of this condition'.

They add this information to complete John's ABC:

A – Activating Event:
- Trigger: his current bout of Depression
- Inference/danger: that he was stupid; weak; weird; worthless and a failure.
B – Belief/Demands:
- 'Because I have clinical depression and cannot get rid

of it by myself, I am weak, weird, useless, a failure and worthless.' 'I should not have to put up with the discomfort and disturbance of this condition.'

C – Consequences:

- Emotional reactions: depression and frustration
- Physical reactions: fatigue; poor concentration; difficulties with memory, sleep, appetite and motivation
- Behaviour: withdrawing socially; breaking off current relationship; ruminating; drinking excessively; eating poorly; spending too much time in bed; considering self-harm.

John now has a clearer understanding of how his thinking and behaviour have been negatively affected by his clinical depression.

Dr Jim then explains that there is little point in trying to challenge his emotions. 'That is just the way we feel about something,' he explains, 'and it is a pointless exercise trying to feel differently. However, we can learn a lot by exploring and challenging your unhealthy thinking and behavioural patterns.'

They begin challenging John's behaviours: were they in any way assisting him in relation to his current situation? How could withdrawing socially, for example, or drinking more, ceasing exercise, eating poorly or considering self-harm, assist the situation? They discuss healthier alternatives.

Dr Jim begins to challenge John's irrational beliefs and demands. 'Is it rational or irrational,' he asks, 'to believe that you are useless or worthless or weak or weird or stupid?'

John admits that up to this point, he had always believed that these 'labels' were indeed true. This leads to a life-changing conversation, with Dr Jim challenging John as to whether human beings could be defined or rated in such a manner. When John hesitates to answer this, Dr Jim asks him to perform the Rating Exercise described earlier, with John's personal rating coming in at around twenty on the scale though he believed that others would rate him much higher at around seventy.

'Where would you rate yourself, John, when you find yourself struggling with a bout of depression, and where do you believe that others would rate you if they learned of your difficulties?' asks Dr Jim.

John replies that his personal rating would drop to five and that others would reduce their rating to thirty!

'But can a human being be rated or measured in such a manner at all?' asks Dr Jim. He then admits that the exercise was a trick. 'Human beings are too special, wonderful and unique,' he continues, 'to be boxed in and measured like commodities in this manner.'

On further discussion, they agree that the only part of the human being which could be rated is in practice their behaviour or skills and talents.

This leads to a discussion on how all of us have an internal critic which Dr Jim calls the pathological critic. 'This is the voice in your head, which is so self-critical of everything we say and do,' he explains further. 'The voice which makes you believe that you are worthless, or useless, or a failure.'

John could relate to this voice as it had been with him since childhood, but he recognised it had been rampant since his bout of depression had begun.

Dr Jim explains how our childhood and adolescent experiences can inform this negative, internally self-destructive bully, which can cause us so much distress. In clinical depression, he explains further, 'The emotional brain can run riot, assigning negativity to all aspects of both ourselves and our lives. Normally, the rational brain can put manners on it, but during a bout of Depression, it is sidelined.'

John comments that since starting to take antidepressants this critical internal voice had lost some of its power but was still causing him distress.

Dr Jim then introduces John to the world of Unconditional Self-Acceptance where he would challenge himself to become comfortable in his own skin, by learning to accept himself as the special and unique human being that he is. To achieve this, he would have to cease rating or judging himself or allowing others to do so but would be free to rate and take responsibility for his behaviour.

He asks John to perform the Unconditional Self-Acceptance Exercise, mentioned earlier in this chapter, for the next three months. He is to carry a notebook for three months, and anytime he finds himself rating himself as a failure or useless or worthless, etc., he is to write down the trigger and his rating. Then later, on paper, he has to challenge the rating as discussed earlier. John, quite taken by the idea, agrees to put this exercise into practice.

Dr Jim then briefly challenges John's demand that 'he should not have to put up with the discomfort of this condition'.

'Is this demand rational or irrational?' he asks.

John believes that it is completely rational, 'Why should I have to put up with this discomfort?'

This leads to a discussion on whether the world would change to suit John and whether we can dodge discomfort in life. He is forced to accept eventually that these demands are irrational and that all of us are going to experience some form of physical or psychological conditions, whether we like it or not. John finds it of assistance when Dr Jim likens clinical depression to diabetes or migraine. Even though John's bout of depression was an unpleasant experience, others too, he now accepts, have their own trials to bear.

Nine months later, John is in a new place. His bout of clinical depression has cleared. He is off medication and taking care of his lifestyle. He has successfully, with the assistance of his tutor, passed his college exams and is now considering doing a Masters. He had recommenced his romance with Jill, who had been a constant companion on his journey towards recovery.

With the assistance of the Unconditional Self-Acceptance Exercise, he was increasingly comfortable in his own skin and was now a mental-health ambassador in the college, assisting others who found themselves struggling with Depression or self-harm. He accepted that there was always the possibility in the future that he might experience another episode but felt that he now had the knowledge and the tools to deal with such an eventuality. Emotionally, he was healed.

PART THREE

Shame and Guilt

4. Shame

Would you like to deal with those nagging feelings of shame or embarrassment triggered by something which is going on in your life at present, or connected to some secrets from your past which you would prefer remained hidden? Are you prone to being affected by what others, in your mind, think of you as a person, but would love to learn how to be otherwise? If you can relate to the above, then read on, for this chapter is going to delve into the shadowy world of shame.

What is Shame?

Shame is a deeply felt, socially driven, painful emotion, whereby we believe that we are perceived by others as being inferior, unworthy of their respect or deserving of their contempt, possibly due to actions which we personally, or as part of a group, have taken. We can also feel shame if we break internal codes of conduct, which we hold dear and judge ourselves accordingly. This is sometimes called internal shame.

It is a natural progression to move from depression to shame. Because shame is linked to a belief that you must accept the negative ratings of others, it is commonly linked with the emotion of depression, where you are applying such negative personal ratings to yourself. This is because depression the emotion has at its heart the belief that I as a human being can be measured, rated or judged by myself as being inferior or worthless, in comparison to others. It is a natural progression from this to the equally irrational belief that I can be measured, rated or judged by others in a similar manner.

From an evolutionary perspective, humans are strongly socially driven creatures, with a deep-seated fear of being ostracized by the group. This explains why shame is so often associated with fear or anxiety, with the commonest example of this being social anxiety, discussed in chapter two.

Shame is also commonly linked with, and often confused with, the emotion of guilt, which we will be discussing in the next chapter.

Psychologists sometimes alternate the terms shame and embarrassment. The latter is perceived as being less intense and linked more with messing up publicly or the fear of doing so. Shame is regarded as being a more intense feeling, involving the whole self, which does not require any obvious public mistake or display to be triggered. For the purposes of this chapter, I do not intend to split these two terms up, believing such distinctions to be arbitrary and of little value, so will fuse them together under the wider umbrella of shame.

Common Causes of Shame

There are countless potential causes or triggers for this emotion.

If struggling with shame, you may see yourself in some of the following:

1. You may be ashamed of some aspects of your upbringing. This might involve coming from socially deprived areas, having a history of family members involved in the criminal world or who have spent time in jail, hiding a background of addiction or a family history of severe mental-health difficulties or a history of domestic or family violence and so on.

2. You may be ashamed of your body image. Body-image issues are also becoming an increasing issue in our Instagram-driven world, where others' assessment of your 'image' (whatever that may be) can trigger shame. You may feel obsessed and ashamed about what others will think of your personal appearance.

3. You may find yourself in debt, or are aware financial difficulties are coming down the tracks. Perhaps you have made some poor financial decisions and are struggling with lenders such as banks or mortgage companies or debt collectors. You may be hiding such information from spouses or family and fear that this information may become known to both them and the wider public. Shame can also occur at a company level, where you are in deep financial trouble and trying to maintain a public profile that all is well, but fear that this might become known to all. All of the above may place a considerable strain on your mental health, with increased risks of self-harm.

4. You may be the victim of social-media shaming, which is an increasing consequence of the current poorly regulated industry. This may involve the sharing of sexually explicit photos or videos of you online, by ex-partners or trolls who want to shame you publicly. Sometimes

such images may have been artificially tweaked to make it seem as if you were involved in something which you were not. It can also take the form of cyberbullying, where groups, sometimes known to the victim, publicly mock and attempt to shame you publicly online. Once again, there is a high risk of self-harm in those vulnerable to this occurrence. Some social-media platforms, such as Instagram, Twitter, Facebook and others, can be associated with this 'mob' social-media shaming culture.

5. You may be the victim of sexual abuse, sexual assault, rape or of domestic abuse (male or female) or violence. This in my experience can be a powerful trigger for a lifelong battle with shame. We will meet Anne later and see how she overcame her struggles in this area.

6. You may be one of the one in six couples who have struggled with infertility issues and are fighting a battle with shame, believing that others in society are judging you for not having children. I have seen this as a crushing cause of deep-seated shame for some women, often associated with the emotion of depression.

7. You may be someone who has not had the good fortune to have met someone to spend the rest of your life with and feel ashamed as to what others think of you as a result. Or you may be struggling with loneliness and ashamed to admit how difficult you are finding this battle, for fear of what others might think.

8. You may be struggling with a mental-health condition, such as major depression, bipolar disorder, psychosis, OCD or an eating disorder. Shame is the emotion which underlies the stigma underlying such conditions and

which I have spent my life trying to challenge, on behalf of all these groups.

9. There is one group which is often overlooked, namely those who suffer from severe PTSD, especially those who have spent time in the military or in front-line services. I wonder how many ex-soldiers, for example, in the UK and USA, have died by suicide, directly due to the feelings of shame, self-contempt and a fear that others would discover some of the awful things they may have seen or done as part of their job. Is shame one of the hidden underlying triggers for the epidemic of suicides in this group?

10. You may struggle with social anxiety. This can take the form of performance anxiety where you are ashamed as to what others will think of you if you mess up during a work or college presentation, public talk, wedding speech or so on. Or you may find yourself ashamed at what others will think of you in social interactional situations, which we dealt with in the chapter on anxiety.

11. You may be struggling with a hidden addiction, with gambling perhaps being the most insidious and destructive. Such addictions also can relate to alcohol, online gambling, drugs (legal and illegal) or sex. I have seen some tragic consequences when such addictions lead to potential ruin for the person and families involved. Rather than face the judgements which may ensue, self-harm may be the behaviour chosen to deal with the shame which has been triggered.

12. You may be someone who has messed up in some way in your past, often sexually. You may have been sexually promiscuous at an earlier age and are now ashamed of

both your behaviour and what people will think if they find out. You may have had an affair or got drunk at a work party and had sex with a co-worker, or behaved foolishly or made a fool of yourself when drunk. You may be ashamed that you are gay and have not 'come out'. Thankfully here in Ireland as a result of the recent referendum on gay marriage, this is becoming less of an issue. You may have used drugs in adolescence and are now ashamed that this information will become public knowledge. Once again, some of these scenarios can lead to intense emotional distress and suicide.

This is only a cross-section of a myriad of potentially triggering causes of shame. They cover the whole gamut of life, which explains why I believe this emotion is more prevalent than generally perceived. If you can see yourself in this list and are struggling with shame, read on.

The Potential Consequences of Shame

This emotion is destructive and can lead to potentially damaging consequences.

1. Shame is damaging to our mental health, as it is perceived by the emotional brain and the body as a threat. This in turn can lead to increased levels of anxiety. Because shame exposes us to the world of personal self- and other-rating, it can also trigger bouts of clinical depression in those who are at risk.
2. The major risk occurs when you believe (whatever the trigger happens to be, whether sexual, financial or otherwise),

that the judgement that will be heaped upon you by family, friends or 'society' if your secret becomes public will be absolutely damning. You may then see suicide or self-harm as the only route out of the judgement and shame that will follow. This is of course untrue, as there is always a healthier option. Alas, many people travel down this dark road. For me, this is a tragic loss of wonderful lives, for as we will explore later, a change in thinking and behaviour can often eliminate this emotion from your life, without destroying the lives of those you leave behind.

3. Shame can also damage relationships, if one or other party is not sharing with the other the source of their shame, but is clearly emotionally distressed.

4. It can damage our work prospects. This is especially the case in presentation anxiety, where I have known highly skilled people refuse possible promotions in major companies and academically, due to the necessity of having to do presentations as part of their upscaling. They do this to avoid the shame of what others might think of them if they were to mess up such presentations.

How to Manage the Emotion of Shame

You experience the emotion of shame when you believe irrationally that others will discover something negative about you and judge you accordingly, and that you must accept their judgement. We have already discussed typical 'shame triggers' that might lead to this false belief being unleashed into your emotional mind. In the previous chapter we explored how your internal critic is adept at making you falsely believe that you are a failure, useless, worthless, etc. and should be avoided by people. What happens in shame is that you believe that others will apply the same critical judgements of you – i.e. that you are a failure, useless, abnormal, worthless – if such shame triggers are made public. The threat of this happening is what makes us anxious in such situations.

It is the world of self- and other-rating which lies at the heart of shame. If you believe that you as a human being can be rated at all, then trouble beckons. As already discussed, the only part of you that can be rated, measured or judged is your behaviour, including your skills and talents.

If you wish to escape the clutches of shame, I advise you to take the following steps.

The first is to develop Unconditional Self-Acceptance, where you cease rating yourself as a human being or allowing others to do so, but accept responsibility for your behaviour. The latter is important as all of us regularly make mistakes or mess up in relation to our actions. It is part of who we are as human beings. Such mistakes, however, do not define who we are as a person!

The second is to explore the unhealthy behaviours which may be worsening and consolidating this unhealthy, negative emotion. They may also be damaging you personally, and, in the case of self-harm, others who love you.

Let's visit firstly with Claire and then Anne, both of whom struggled with shame, and see how they learned how to emotionally self-heal.

Claire's Story

Claire is a thirty-nine-year-old business executive, married to Simon for five years. They have been trying to conceive for the previous three years. Every avenue to date has failed, including three trials of IVF. Claire is referred to Dr Jim for assistance, having become increasingly emotionally distressed due to the situation, which was creating personal and relationship difficulties with Simon.

Dr Jim listens empathetically and offers to assist her in managing these issues by using some CBT techniques. He explains about rational and irrational beliefs and lays out the ABC concepts, explaining how they will employ this system to locate and manage her irrational beliefs. They decide to use her 'failure to conceive' as the trigger.

'And how did this make you feel emotionally?' asks Dr Jim.

'I felt depressed and ashamed,' she replies.

'What were your behavioural responses to these emotions?' asks Dr Jim. 'What did you do when you felt like this?'

Claire admits to avoiding siblings and friends with children of their own, for fear they would bring up the subject of when she would have a baby of her own. She had avoided informing anyone that she had had IVF because she was afraid they would think she was a failure for being unable to conceive naturally. She also admits to increasing social isolation, ruminating about her situation and worrying about others finding out about her secret difficulties.

'And how did these emotions make you feel physically?' asks Dr Jim.

'I felt tired and struggled with motivation and concentration,' Claire replies.

Dr Jim then begins to explore what inferences she had taken from her difficulties in conception that led her to experience her emotions of depression and especially shame. He begins by asking Claire, 'What was it about your difficulties with conceiving that caused you to feel depressed?'

'I am such a failure,' she replies, 'useless to Simon or myself as I am unable to conceive like normal women.'

'And ashamed?' Dr Jim asks.

'What would others think of me?' she replies. 'I can sense their unspoken criticism of me, in comments made about other couples our age already having children. That it is time for me to stop living the high life and have a family. Subtle hints are coming from both siblings and friends, none of whom I have informed about my current difficulties.'

'Let's examine what irrational beliefs were triggered by your difficulties with conception and the inferences you assigned to them,' says Dr Jim. 'This usually takes the form of some absolute demands you were making about the trigger, which in this case is your difficulties with conception.'

With Dr Jim's assistance and after some detailed discussions, Claire decides that her belief in relation to her emotion of depression was 'that because she was unable to conceive, she was a failure and useless'. They also agree that her belief in relation to her emotion of shame was 'that others would discover her secret, that she was infertile, and judge her as a failure and useless, and that she would have to accept their judgement.'

Claire's ABC looked like this:

A – Activating Event:
- Trigger: difficulties in conceiving
- Inference/danger: that I am a failure and useless; others might discover that I am struggling to conceive and would judge me as a failure and useless.

B – Belief/Demands:
- 'Because I am unable to conceive, I am a failure and useless.' 'Others will discover my secret difficulties in conceiving, judge me and I must accept their judgement.'

C – Consequences:

- Emotional reactions: depression and shame
- Physical reactions: fatigue; poor concentration; poor motivation
- Behaviour: withdrawing socially; ruminating; avoiding siblings and close friends and acquaintances who have children; avoiding any discussion around the topic of children.

Dr Jim then challenges Claire's behaviour. They agree that withdrawing socially or hiding away from contact with siblings or friends with children, or avoiding discussion about IVF, was only adding to her difficulties. Things would have to change and she accepts that several frank conversations need to be had with family, friends and loved ones.

Dr Jim then challenges Claire's irrational beliefs and demands. He is especially interested in her belief that 'she was a failure and useless'.

'Is this a rational or irrational belief?' he asks.

This leads to an important discussion in which Claire comes to a realisation with his assistance, and following the Rating Exercise, that human beings cannot be rated or measured in such a manner. Dr Jim then assists her to challenge her belief that 'she must accept the negative judgements of others'. Claire, after some arguments, accepts that this, too, is both irrational and unhelpful, for the same reasons.

They discuss her inner 'critic' and how this voice has been destroying her internal peace and calm, by pouring out its venomous comments that 'she was a failure and useless'.

This leads to a chat as to whether she was allowing others to judge her in a similar manner to her inner critic, with Claire now accepting that she was simply 'loaning out her pathological critic to others, to beat herself up with'.

Dr Jim then introduces her to the world of Unconditional Self-Acceptance where she would learn to become comfortable in her own skin by accepting herself as the special unique human being that she is. To achieve this, she would have to cease rating or judging herself or allowing others to do so. They both agree that doing so would assist her to eliminate her emotions of depression and shame, whilst remaining free to rate and take responsibility for her behaviour. He asks her to perform the Unconditional Self-Acceptance exercise, mentioned earlier in this chapter, for the following three months and Claire readily agrees.

Finally, and following a frank discussion, they agree that she had done everything in her power to conceive a baby and that the results which followed were completely out of her control and rested with Mother Nature. But, irrespective of whether successful or not, Claire had to cease playing the rating game, either with herself or others.

Six months later, Claire's life is transformed. She has ceased rating herself and allowing others to do so. Courtesy of performing the Self-Acceptance Exercise regularly, she is now comfortable in her own skin. She has informed everyone close to her about her current difficulties and is amazed at the empathy and support she receives, some even confiding in her about their experiences in the same area. She has now come to an acceptance that if it is meant to be, then it would happen and if not, she is still a lucky lady to have Simon in her life. Her emotions of depression and shame fade away. Nine months later, she attends Dr Jim to let him know that one final IVF trial has been successful, and she is now four months pregnant.

Anne's Story

Anne is referred by her family doctor to see Dr Jim following a failed suicide attempt. She is in her mid-thirties and works as a hotel receptionist. She is single and deeply unhappy. On every occasion when a relationship became too close, she would shut it down. Although extremely attractive, she purposely played down her physical appearance at every opportunity. She found herself increasingly lonely and drank heavily to blot out the deep-seated emotional pain and self-hatred, which had dogged her life from the age of fourteen, when she was raped by an 'upstanding member' of her local community, who has since passed away. She was deeply ashamed of what occurred and convinced that nobody would believe her story. The pain and self-hatred gradually became too much for her to bear, and Anne took a massive overdose to eliminate the source of her pain, which she believed to be herself.

Following weeks in hospital, Anne survives but hides the cause of her emotional distress from the specialist and nurses trying to assist her. She does, however, reveal all to her family doctor. Anne is not ready to attend rape crisis or other counselling services but agrees to attend Dr Jim, on her GP's advice, to find a path out of her current difficulties.

She breaks down in front of Dr Jim. He listens empathetically to her story and offers to assist her to manage these issues by using some CBT techniques. He explains about rational and irrational beliefs and lays out the ABC concepts, explaining how they will employ this system to locate and manage her irrational beliefs. They decide to use her rape as the trigger.

'And how did this make you feel emotionally?' asks Dr Jim.

'I felt depressed and ashamed,' she replies.

'What was your behavioural responses to these emotions?' asks Dr Jim. 'What did you do when you felt like this?'

Anne admits to years of hiding behind a 'smokescreen' which she put up as a façade to blot the world out. She never allowed men to get too close, especially sexually. She purposely down-played her appearances on every occasion. She had also hidden all details of her rape, from family and friends, dreading that they would somehow find out her secret. She also admits to years of self-hatred and using alcohol to blot out the emotional pain, and to her failed suicide attempt.

'And physically?' asks Dr Jim.

Anne reveals years of fatigue, sleep difficulties, nightmares and flashbacks, and how she struggles to enjoy life or become joyous about anything.

They add this information to Anne's ABC:

A – Activating Event:
- Trigger: raped at the age of fourteen
- Inference/danger:
B – Belief/Demands:
C – Consequences:
- Emotional reactions: depression and shame
- Physical reactions: fatigue; anhedonia; poor motivation
- Behaviour: hiding rape from family and friends; with-drawing socially; not allowing men to get too close sexually or otherwise; dressing down purposefully in relation to body image and gear; suicide attempt.

Dr Jim then explores what inferences that she had taken from her rape that led her to experience her emotions of depression and shame. He begins by asking Anne: 'What was it about your rape that caused you to feel depressed?'

'I am worthless' she replies, with tears streaming down her face.

'I am of no value to myself or anyone else, especially men. I also feel that because of what happened that I am ugly and abnormal.'

'And why ashamed?' Dr Jim asks.

'What would others think of me?' she replies. 'I feel debased and degraded as a human being and know that they would look down on me as "used goods" and someone to be shunned if they discovered what happened. I fear most that they would pity me,' she adds. 'I just could not bear their judgement.'

Dr Jim empathises with her but suggests that they might examine what irrational beliefs were triggered by her rape and the inferences she assigned to it. 'This usually takes the form of some absolute demands you were making about the trigger, which in this case was the rape,' he adds.

With Dr Jim's assistance and after some tear-filled discussions, Anne decides that her belief in relation to her emotion of depression was 'that because she was raped, she was worthless, ugly and abnormal'. They also agree that her belief in relation to her emotion of shame was 'that others would discover her secret (that she had been raped) and judge her accordingly, and that she would have to accept their negative judgements.'

They add this to Anne's ABC:

A – Activating Event:
- Trigger: raped at the age of fourteen
- Inference/danger: that I am used goods; I am ugly and worthless and abnormal; others will judge me as above; they will pity me.

B – Belief/Demands:
- 'Because I was raped, I am worthless, ugly and abnormal.' 'Others might learn of my rape and judge me negatively and I must accept their judgement.'

C – Consequences:

- Emotional reactions: depression and shame
- Physical reactions: fatigue; anhedonia; poor motivation
- Behaviour: hiding rape from family and friends; withdrawing socially; not allowing men to get too close sexually or otherwise; dressing down purposefully in relation to body image and gear; suicide attempt.

Now Anne has a clearer picture of why the rape was causing her so much distress and emotional pain.

'But how can I learn to deal with it?' she asks.

Dr Jim explains that they will have to challenge and reshape her thinking and behaviour to achieve this objective. They begin with her behaviour. Anne agrees that her decades of concealment, social withdrawal, pushing men away, purposely denigrating her body image and appearances and self-harm attempt were only making her emotional difficulties greater. She resolves to begin changing these behaviours by working to improve her relationship with her body image and appearance, ceasing any further self-harm attempts and beginning to reintegrate socially.

Dr Jim then challenges Anne's irrational beliefs and demands, especially her belief that 'she was worthless, ugly and abnormal'.

'Is this a rational or irrational belief?' he asks.

Anne vehemently argues that in her case it is quite rational to believe so. Dr Jim asks her to perform the Rating Exercise, which challenges Anne's perceptions as she gradually comes to an understanding that human beings cannot be rated or measured in such a manner. This leads to a long discussion on the role of her inner critic, how it has been formed and informed by her rape and how it was the source of her belief that she was worthless, ugly and abnormal. A light bulb goes off in Anne's head as she realizes how this bullying voice has been running and destroying her life since she was a teenager. She vows to take on the bully.

Dr Jim then assists her to challenge her belief that 'she must accept the negative judgements of others'. Anne now accepts that this, too, is both irrational and unhelpful. She finds it helpful when Dr Jim explains that she is simply 'loaning out her inner critic to others, to beat herself up with'.

Dr Jim then introduces her to the world of Unconditional Self-Acceptance, where she would learn to become comfortable in her own skin by accepting herself as the special unique human being that she is. To achieve this, she would have to cease rating or judging herself or allowing others to do so, which would eliminate her emotions of depression and shame, but would be free to rate and take responsibility for her behaviour.

He asks Anne to perform the Unconditional Self-Acceptance exercise, mentioned earlier, for the following three months and she agrees to put it into practice.

What follows over the following six months is life-changing for Anne. With assistance from Dr Jim and months of dedicated hard work at taking on her inner critic, she learns how to become increasingly comfortable in her own skin. She agrees, on his advice, to engage in some counselling to deal with her rape, which she finds of great assistance. She decides to inform her family and a few close friends about what happened in her childhood and finds this a cathartic experience, where the love, understanding, tears and empathy she receives from all blows her away. Anne realises that many of the false beliefs that she would be judged negatively by others were untrue. Of greater importance, she no longer cares what others might think of her as a person as she had learned to be at peace with the beautiful, special person that she is.

With these internal changes come great emotional healing and a concomitant decision to prioritise herself physically. She begins to take an interest in how she looks, finds herself a new wardrobe and begins to fully engage in potential relationships. A year later, her hard work bears fruit as she meets Larry, a kind, loving, gentle man who she is happy to commit to.

Key Learning Points

1. Shame is a deep-seated internally powerful, unhealthy negative emotion which has the capacity to cause significant emotional distress in your life.
2. At the heart of shame lies the irrational belief that other people have the power to judge you negatively as a person and that you must accept this judgement.
3. To deal with shame, you must change the irrational belief behind it and also the negative behaviours, which follow in its wake.
4. To change your thinking requires you to develop Unconditional Self-Acceptance, where you cease negatively self-rating yourself as a person or allowing others to do the same, whilst remaining free to challenge your behaviour.
5. You will also have to confront and change many of the unhealthy behavioural consequences which have grown up around this emotion.

5. Guilt

Do you sometimes wish that you could turn back the clock to change the outcome of some decisions made in the past? Are you often plagued by regrets? Do the actions of your past affect your perceptions of the present and even your future? If the answer is yes, let me assure you that it is possible to release yourself from guilt and restore your inner sense of peace.

What is Guilt?

Guilt is a classic unhealthy negative emotion or feeling engendered by the belief that something you have done (or have omitted to do) has caused harm or distress to others. Many of us are familiar with the healthy negative emotion of remorse, for actions which we would prefer not to have engaged in, but for which we have forgiven ourselves. The difference with guilt is that we are unable to forgive ourselves for some action or behaviour, so have a life-long stick to beat ourselves up with.

Guilt is often confused with shame, which we dealt with in the previous chapter, but there are clear differences between both. Shame, as we discussed, is an intensely internally felt emotion triggered by the risk of others finding out something about us and judging us negatively. Guilt does not require, in principle, any form of self- or other-rating, although I have always believed that there is an implied but rarely expressed negative personal self-rating present. Guilt, however, is more related to the consequences of actions which you have or have not taken, and how these have impinged on others. It is possible for both guilt and shame to occur together in response to some negative trigger, which can create a high-risk scenario. Some high-flying bankers and businessmen, for example, have died due to a combination of guilt and shame, secondary to some poor decision making.

Guilt is a destructive emotion which can wear down your emotional reserves over time, and is regularly linked with emotions of anxiety and depression.

It can be both a trigger for and a response to bouts of clinical depression. This emotion is also common in OCD and addiction. It can also lead, unfortunately, to serious self-harm and suicide attempts, where the person can see no way out of the crisis of guilt they have created. Above all, this emotion is renowned for making you feel miserable, unable to enjoy many aspects of life as you believe that you no longer deserve to allow yourself to do so.

Common Guilt Triggers

As with shame, there are multiple opportunities in life that can trigger this emotion. It is impossible to cover them all, but here are some of the most common culprits.

1. Relationship Triggers – These can include one party in a relationship having affair(s), often unknown to the other.

This can engender years of guilt, which can destroy relationships. Or spending too much time at work to the detriment of a personal relationship. Or not visiting or keeping in contact with an elderly parent or relative who subsequently dies.

2. Financial Triggers – These can be a powerful cause of guilt. You may, for example, make poor financial decisions, either domestically or as part of your job or company, leading to financial implosion in either domain, with major consequences for those involved. How many of us have made extremely poor financial decisions with sometimes disastrous consequences?

3. Abuse Triggers – You may feel guilty at either not noticing, stopping or intervening sufficiently in past situations where someone close to you was being abused.

4. Accident Triggers – These can be another powerful trigger for guilt. They may relate to beliefs that you either caused or could have avoided some circumstances where another person was seriously injured or died as a result of an accident or mishap.

5. Survivor Guilt – This is common in those who survive major accidents and in those working in the military or front-line services, where colleagues or friends die and we survive. The guilt involved is often based on completely irrational underlying beliefs but can be amazingly difficult to shift. This is a common cause of suicide in these groups and is often associated with PTSD. Another high-risk group involves the family members and close friends of those who die by suicide, as we will discuss later, in the section on grief.

How to Manage the Emotion of Guilt

If you are struggling with guilt, let's now explore what underlies it and how best to manage it. At the heart of guilt lies the fixed, irrational belief that you ought to have known what was going to happen when you made a particular decision, and as a result should have made a different one. There are two parts to this irrational belief. Firstly, you believe that you should have known in advance all the negative consequences that such a decision was going to cause, especially for those on whom it impinged negatively. Secondly, that you should not have made such a decision in the first place. Because you cannot change the decision that you made, there seems to be no way out of the conundrum. This can be an extremely fixed belief, and difficult to shift.

It is not only the irrational belief underlying your guilt which is causing you difficulties, it is also how you may behave as a result of your guilt. You may spend countless hours ruminating and agonising as to what else you could have done. What you are really trying to do here (as my friend and colleague CBT therapist Enda Murphy often comments) is to rewrite the script of what happened. Imagine a film director who, six months after their film was panned by the critics, is now reviewing the film. They now notice that there were several scenes which they would have preferred to shoot differently. They long to rewrite the script and reshoot the scenes. Alas, the main players and crew are scattered to the four winds. You can see that it would be impossible for them to recreate what has already passed. Can you also see that the same may be true for whatever situation you are trying to resolve?

You may also be avoiding meeting up with those whom you believe have been impacted by your decision, or those who remind you of the effects of the decision. You may be constantly trying to make up for the mistakes you believe you made, which can place immense stress on your emotional reserves. You may be drinking too much to blot out your inner guilt and pain. You may consider or act out some self-harm attempts in situations where you believe that the damage done is irreparable. In such scenarios, you are attempting to punish yourself for what you believe you have done.

If you wish to banish this unhealthy, negative emotion, you need to do the following:

1. You must challenge the demand that you should have known what was going to happen and should not have done it. The reality is that none of us can see into the future. When making a decision we cannot anticipate what, if any, potentially negative consequences might ensue. Suppose you decide to put all your finances into what seems to be a wonderful business venture. Then, due to unforeseen world events, there is a financial crash and you lose most of your venture capital. This leads to unexpected consequences for your family and business colleagues. Could you really have anticipated that all this was going to happen? The answer, of course, is no. Imagine that you were to avoid making any decision in life, unless absolutely certain of the outcome and potential consequences. You would never make any decision at all. The reality, of course, is that it is pointless to keep revisiting the past, because you cannot undo what has already been done.

2. You must also challenge and change the negative behavioural patterns which may have grown up around your guilt, such as ruminations, constantly demanding that things work out differently, avoiding people and

situations which remind you of your perceived mistake, self-medicating with alcohol, passing your emotion of guilt on to new situations or self-harm attempts. None of these will change one iota the irrational belief behind guilt, or the negative outcomes which may have occurred due to some decision which you have made. Beating yourself up constantly because of the latter is both unhelpful and a waste of time.

Let's now meet Alan, who has been struggling with guilt for years, and see how he learns to emotionally heal himself, by changing his thinking and behaviour.

Alan's Story

Alan attends Dr Jim after a long battle with emotional distress. Following a heavy bout of drinking, he has made a serious suicide attempt. A forty-three-year-old plumber, he is married to Jenny, with whom he shares two adored daughters. Thanks to the intervention of Jenny, he survives the suicide attempt. Filled with remorse for his actions, Alan agrees to explore the cause of his emotional distress with Dr Jim. Breaking down, he reveals that fifteen years earlier, his best friend Mick had died by suicide.

Alan had learned to cope with the sadness and loss following his death, but simply couldn't handle the guilt. It had eaten him alive for years. Even Jenny was unaware of how intense his emotion of guilt was. Hardly a day passed without him beating himself up for his role in the tragedy. The guilt was now seeping into other areas of his life.

Dr Jim listens empathetically to his story and offers to assist Alan to manage his guilt by using some CBT techniques. He explains about rational and irrational beliefs and lays out the ABC concepts, explaining how they will employ this system to locate and manage his irrational beliefs. They decide to use Mick's suicide as the trigger.

'And how did this make you feel emotionally?' asks Dr Jim.

'I felt so guilty,' he replies. 'Initially I was numb and then overcome with sadness and pain, but it was the guilt which haunted me most and continues to do so.'

He had learned to accept his friend's loss as the years had progressed, even if he missed him greatly, but was still struggling to deal with his guilt.

'What were your behavioural responses to this emotion of guilt?' asks Dr Jim. 'What did you do when you felt like this?'

Alan reveals years of unhealthy behaviours which had grown up around his guilt. How he refused to discuss Alan's death with anyone, even Jenny or close friends. How he ruminated and emotionally beat himself up daily. How, when Jenny was asleep at night, he would spend hours reliving the event and his role in it. How he tried to blot out the guilt with bouts of heavy drinking, which made him feel worse. Finally, his guilt had led to a suicide attempt, which made him feel even more guilty as it had upset Jenny, his family and friends. Again, he broke down as he revisited the potential effects of that decision, which he now realises would have destroyed the future lives of his wife and two daughters.

They add this information to Alan's ABC:

A – Activating Event:
- Trigger: his close friend's suicide
- Inference/danger:
B – Belief/Demands:
C – Consequences:
- Emotional reactions: guilt

- Behaviour: refuses to discuss his friend's suicide with friends or family; constantly ruminates daily and when in bed over his role in his death; drinks excessively to blot out the guilt; self-harm attempt.

Dr Jim then asks: 'What was it about your friend's death by suicide that is causing you to feel so guilty?'

'Because I could have prevented it,' replies Alan.

He then reveals his role in the events which led up to the day when Mick died by suicide. They had known each other since childhood and were inseparable. After leaving school, Mick became an electrician and Alan a plumber. They continued to socialise regularly, even playing together for the local football team.

Mick always seemed to be on good form, constantly joking and laughing with Alan, and his friends and workmates. He had been going out with a local girl, Linda, for several years. All seemed well in his world.

Several days before Mick died, he revealed to Alan that he was feeling a little down as things were not going so well with Linda. He was afraid that she was about to break up their relationship. Alan reassured him that it was probably only a phase, and that they would get through it. Mick seemed to cheer up following this conversation.

Unfortunately for Alan, he was especially busy in the days which followed this conversation. Mick did try to contact him on one occasion, but Alan texted back, explaining that he was busy at work and that he would catch up with him the following Saturday in the pub. On the day Mick died, Alan was dealing with a sudden emergency where a tank had overflowed in a house. He missed another call from Mick as a result.

Later, Alan would get what turned out to be a final text from

Mick, saying, 'Sorry, mate', but he only read it after the event. For Mick hanged himself that afternoon.

Dr Jim empathizes with Alan as to how distressing this must have been for him but probes further. 'What is it about what happened that makes you feel so guilty about his death?'

'If I had only realized how distressed he was,' Alan replies. 'I could have intervened and saved him.'

'But was he showing evidence of being extremely distressed?' asks Dr Jim.

'In retrospect, he wasn't,' he replies. 'But I was his best mate and should have known that he was in trouble.'

'Is there anything else about what happened that is causing you to feel guilty?' Dr Jim asks.

'I didn't answer his calls, especially the one on the day he died,' replies Alan. 'That distresses me most. He was clearly looking for help and I, his best mate, let him down by not replying to him when he needed me. If I had answered his calls, he might still be alive today'.

'So now let's examine what irrational beliefs were triggered by Mick's death, and the inferences you assigned to it,' says Dr Jim. 'This usually takes the form of some absolute demands you were making about the trigger, which in this case was his suicide.'

Following some discussion, Alan decides that his belief in relation to his friend's suicide was that he should have known that Mick was in difficulty and should have done something to prevent his death. Or, as Dr Jim put it, that 'he should have known what to do and should have done it.'

They add this information to complete Alan's ABC:

A – Activating Event:
- Trigger: his close friend's suicide

- Inference/danger: I didn't recognise that Mick was emotionally distressed; as his best friend I ought to have done so; my failure to answer Mick's call on the day he died was inexcusable; if I had recognised his distress and answered his call, my friend would be alive today.

B – Belief/Demands:

- 'I should have known that Mick was in trouble emotionally and should have intervened to prevent him dying by suicide'. 'I should have understood the significance of, and answered, his call on the day of his suicide.'

C – Consequences:

- Emotional reactions: guilt
- Behaviour: refuses to discuss his friend's suicide with friends or family; constantly ruminates daily and when in bed over his role in his death; drinks excessively to blot out the guilt; self-harm attempt.

Now Alan has a clear picture of why he has been so distressed emotionally since the day his friend had died.

Dr Jim then challenges his behaviour. 'Is this behaviour helping you deal with your guilt?'

Alan accepts that trying to avoid discussing Mick's death with family, friends or colleagues, whilst ruminating on it day and night, was unhealthy and unhelpful, as was his drinking and self-harm attempt. None of these behaviours were assisting him to deal with his guilt but were, on the contrary, adding to his distress. He agrees to challenge them over the months to come.

The real battle begins, though, when Dr Jim challenges Alan's belief that he should have known that Mick was in trouble, answered his calls and prevented his suicide.

'Is this rational or irrational?' Dr Jim asks.

'For me,' Alan replies, 'this is a completely rational and sensible demand.'

'Do you have second sight?' asks Dr Jim.

Alan is confused by this question, until Dr Jim explains that this is a term to describe those who claim to be able to see into the future. This leads to a discussion on how human beings constantly berate themselves after the event for not being able to predict what eventually happens.

'What you are saying,' says Alan, 'is that I could not have been aware as to how distressed Mick was. Or that not answering his calls immediately was going to lead to such a terrible outcome?'

Dr Jim agrees. 'What you are trying to do in retrospect is to rewrite the script of what happened so that the ending would turn out differently.'

He gives Alan the example we saw earlier, of a film director wanting to redo some scenes in a film, long after the actors and actresses have scattered around the globe.

This leads to a discussion on what Dr Jim believes to be lying at the heart of Alan's emotional difficulties. 'Guilt is always about the decision,' he explains, 'and the consequences which flow from that decision. Were you aware, for example, on the day of Mick's death, in the middle of trying to assist a householder to save their house from the damage done by an overflowing tank, of the potential outcome of not answering Mick's calls?'

Alan was starting to see where this discussion was going.

'What you are saying,' he suggests, 'is that the decision that I made at the time, to assist the householder save their house, and to plan to speak to Mick later, was made with the best of intentions as I was unaware of how distressed he was or his plans to take his own life?'

Dr Jim agrees. 'It is easy to be retrospectively hard on ourselves, when a decision such as this does not work out as expected, but we must examine the circumstances surrounding the decision.'

He elaborates further, 'Whenever you make a decision about anything in life, you must accept that you do so based on the information you have at your disposal, and the emotional state that you are in, at that moment in time. You cannot, therefore, castigate yourself subsequently if the consequences of that decision are not what you expected to occur, for yourself or others. If you have made that decision with the best of intentions, then you must learn to let it go and accept that you cannot control all the variables, many of which are unknown, which might lead to such consequences.'

For Alan, this is a light-bulb moment, as he suddenly realizes that he has spent years condemning himself for decisions he had made at the time with the best of intentions, and with no awareness of the depths of emotional distress that Mick had been experiencing.

Over the following months, Alan puts into practice much of what he has learned from his discussions with Dr Jim. He challenges his unhealthy behaviours, especially his silence and alcohol binges. He reveals all to Jenny, who is relieved to know that he has pinpointed the source of his distress and is dealing with it.

Any time Alan found himself slipping back into 'guilt mode' about Mick's death or indeed about other areas of his life, he followed Dr Jim's suggestion and wrote out the pros and cons of any decisions made and the emotional state he was in at the time of their making. He began to become increasingly pragmatic about decisions that he had to make in life, accepting that he could only do the best he could and that he would never be able to control the potential outcomes or consequences.

Finally, Alan spent an emotional half-hour sitting beside Mick's grave, explaining to his friend what had happened and that he was letting his emotion of guilt go. This allowed the sadness and pain of his loss to bubble up to the surface, with tears flowing freely. He felt lighter and freer after this visit. As he reveals to Jenny, he now feels finally healed.

Key Learning Points
1. Guilt is another powerful negative unhealthy emotion, which can be destructive of your peace of mind and lead to significant emotional distress. It is often triggered when some decision you have made leads to negative consequences for others.
2. Underlying this emotion is an irrational belief that, on looking back at your decision, you now believe that you should have known what was going to happen in the future and should have been able to prevent the negative consequences which ensued.
3. Managing this emotion will involve you challenging this irrational belief and the unhealthy behaviours which ensue from it.
4. To change your thinking will involve an acceptance that you do not have the ability to see into the future or to change the outcome of any decision by 'rewriting the script'. You must accept in life that whenever you make a decision, you do so with the information or circumstances pertaining at that time, and the emotional state you are in. You cannot predict the outcome of a decision before you make it, so must learn to let yourself off the hook, forgive yourself and move on.
5. It is also important to change unhealthy behaviours which have grown up around your guilt, as these are damaging both yourself and those around you.

PART FOUR

Hurt and Anger

6. Hurt

Would you like to finally get rid of that 'chip on your shoulder' which is disturbing your inner peace and tranquillity? Would you like to develop some positive insights and techniques to deal with those periods when you experience hurt, believing that others or life are not treating you fairly? Would you like to learn how to become less hypersensitive in your reactions to other people's comments or behaviour? If the answer to any of these questions is yes, read on.

What is Hurt?

Hurt is an unhealthy negative emotion or feeling, engendered by the belief that others are not treating you fairly, *that you are not being treated fairly* or that life is not treating you fairly. Over decades of assisting those in emotional distress, I have found hurt to be one of the commonest, most toxic negative emotions of them all. I often describe it as if those affected are being consumed from the inside out by a caustic acid. For hurt burns all before it, leaving behind what feels like an emotional wilderness. It can harden your heart, making you feel bitter and deeply unhappy. It is commonly associated with the emotion of depression and I have also seen this emotion lead to bouts of severe clinical depression. Hurt is linked to the emotion of frustration, and can create a toxic environment for those you live or work with as it makes you suspicious, prickly and hypersensitive to the smallest of slights. It can lead to you pushing people away emotionally, creating difficulties for your personal and other relationships. Hurt can unfortunately quickly grow legs, with negative consequences accumulating as it spreads its tentacles. Yet it can be addressed and dealt with remarkably swiftly, as you will see.

Hurt is regularly confused in people's minds with anger, which we will be dealing with in the following chapter, but these emotions differ in some important areas, as we will explore later. They can also, in certain situations, overlap, which is why hurt and anger are often described as being two sides of the same coin.

Common Hurt Triggers

As with guilt and shame, there are multiple triggers that can lead to hurt. The following list is only a small sample of the many life situations which can trigger this emotion.

1. Family – This is, in my experience, the most common trigger. You may believe that parents or siblings did not treat you fairly, or that one or other sibling was given preferential treatment, emotionally, financially or otherwise. Countless people believe their childhood to be the source of their current difficulties, feeling they were treated unfairly or denied the perfect childhood they believe others experienced. Or it may be that you, as a parent, believe your children are treating you unfairly.

2. Relationships – These form another large block of potential hurt triggers. Hurt may occur when a relationship breaks down, with one or other party believing that they were treated unfairly and proceeding to carry the grudge into future relationships. It can rear its head in partnerships or marriages, where once again you may believe that you are being unfairly dealt with and react accordingly. In my experience, if hurt begins to intrude upon your life on this front, serious difficulties will arrive in its wake.

3. Bullying – This is another powerful trigger for hurt. Bullying, as we know, can occur at any age and in any context or environment. School is a common place for the early development of this emotion. You may believe that you were being unfairly picked upon or insufficiently protected by parents, teachers, sports coaches or peers. It can occur in families, where siblings, for example, make the lives of their brothers or sisters hell. You may believe that this should not have happened and that, once again, you were unprotected by parents or other older siblings.

4. Workplace – The workplace can unfortunately be a source of significant hurt. This is particularly so if you believe that managers or bosses are treating you differently or unfairly in comparison to work colleagues when it comes to tasks given, or responsibility allotted, not being praised for work done and so on. You might be harassed by other colleagues, without the normal protections being present. Clearly bullying can also surface in this environment and can trigger substantial hurt, if you believe that you are being treated unfairly.

5. Abuse – This can be one of the most destructive triggers for hurt. It most commonly resides around the belief

that you were not protected from physical, emotional or especially sexual abuse, by parents, older siblings or key professionals such as teachers. The combination of hurt, and the sense of being unprotected, together with the physical and psychological effects of abuse, can trigger significant bouts of clinical depression in those at risk.

6. Social Media – As described earlier, the social-media world is unregulated and being the recipient of unkind comments and trolling can be a source of hurt for many. How many lives have been blighted by deep hurt inflicted upon them by such individuals and groups, otherwise known as 'the social-media mob'? Not only adolescents are at risk, but all of us are. If you believe that you are being treated unfairly and that others seem to be enjoying your pain, then hurt can quickly grow legs and take root in your life.

How to Manage the Emotion of Hurt

Let's now explore what underlies hurt and how best to manage it. At the heart of this emotion lies the belief that you should be treated fairly by others and by life itself. While anyone struggling with hurt genuinely believes this belief and demand to be both sensible and rational, the reality is that it is both irrational and impossible to deliver in real life. It would be a wonderful world if all citizens of our planet were treated with kindness, respect and dignity, but sadly the world is not like that. And indeed, we must admit that there are times when we ourselves may not treat others with kindness, respect and dignity. We have to deal with the world as it is – imperfect, complex and difficult – rather than feel cheated of life in a perfect world that does not exist.

Of course, it is rational and acceptable to prefer or wish to be treated fairly by others or life, but in order to be emotionally healthy we must accept that this will often turn out not to be the case. And, crucially, that this is not anyone's fault, it's just how life goes for everyone.

You may be justifiably questioning how this knowledge can assist you in dealing with your personal emotion of hurt. To do so, it will help to grasp some key insights.

1. Hurt is always about carrying a 'personal' grudge (either against an individual or a member of a group such as a managerial team at work) or indeed against life itself, the latter being more common than you might think.

2. The person who suffers most and is affected most by your carrying a grudge is always you. The person who has caused your hurt is usually blissfully unaware of your emotional difficulties and, even if aware, is often oblivious to your pain. Buddha talked of holding a grudge as being like holding a scalding coal with the intention of throwing it at someone else: the one who gets burned is you. So, it is in your interests to drop the grudge in order to heal yourself.

3. Hurt tends to grow legs as time progresses, so the grudge becomes more ingrained and difficult to shift. It also tends to spread its tentacles to other people and situations.

4. Your behaviour, such as lashing out emotionally or being hypersensitive, is a response to carrying this grudge and is going to cause you further difficulties.

5. If you accept the concept of Unconditional Self-Acceptance, discussed at length in previous chapters, then the only part of the human condition or person that you can rate or measure or challenge is your behaviour. You accept that it is unhelpful to rate yourself as a person and

by corollary be rated by, or rate, others personally. You can, however, rate or challenge your own or another's behaviour. As humans, we all mess up regularly and this puts us all on a level playing field. Just as you are entitled to be critical of your own actions, if appropriate, so too are you entitled to be critical of or challenge the actions of others. This concept is key to managing hurt.

What the above means in practice is that you must find a way to drop your grudge or hurt, as it is only harming you and not the person or situation you believe to be the source of your current difficulties. The secret to unlocking the emotion of hurt is accepting that you must drop the 'personal' grudge, but understanding that you remain able to criticize and challenge a person's behaviour or actions.

To manage your hurt, I therefore recommend the following steps:

1. To understand the concept of carrying a grudge, I ask you to try a physical exercise in which you fill a rucksack with rocks, or heavy books, and carry it while out walking for at least an hour. Note how heavy it becomes and the relief felt when you take it off. This is what it is like to carry grudges for life, and to finally let them go.
2. Learn to apply the lessons of Unconditional Self-Acceptance, where you separate who you are as a person from your behaviour and only rate the latter. You then apply the concept in reverse, to the person whom you believe has treated you unfairly. Forgive the person as it assists you, not them, but feel free to challenge and rate their behaviour or actions.

3. Challenge and change unhealthy behaviour patterns that you may have fallen into over the years. Instead of falling into your natural pattern of seeking evidence that everyone is out to get you, look for the opposite. Pay attention to the moments when people are helpful, or kind, or generous. You will find that focusing on the positives will help you let go of your hypersensitivity, sullen silences and verbal outbursts.

4. Learn to challenge the behaviour of others in a constructive manner. Let's suppose that someone says something to you that causes you to feel hurt. If initially you feel like lashing out, perform the Turtle Exercise, where you take five minutes to 'go into your shell' and only then proceed. This may involve a trip to the rest room or to make a cup of coffee. Then, when you have gained some space and perspective, question the behaviour. Address the behaviour rather than the individual. For example, 'It hurts my feelings when you ignore me in front of others,' rather than 'You always ignore me because you're selfish.' Make the person understand that their actions have caused you to feel upset or hurt and explain why, without attacking them as a person.

Normally this will be all you will have to do.

Occasionally you may have to take the 'nuclear option' and face the person with the consequences of their behaviour. This might involve choosing to remove someone from your life, or raising matters with bosses at work, for example. Remember that you have the choice as to whether to use this option or not, but that you are now the person in charge of this decision.

You may hold a grudge against your mother-in-law, for example, if she is constantly running you down. It is absolutely fine to challenge her behaviour when she criticises you. But the nuclear option of removing her from your life may not be the ideal one to take, even if it seems desirable at the time. What matters when it comes to emotional healing is that you understand your right to challenge the behaviour in this way if you wish. Then, with that understanding, you may choose, for the sake of your relationship, to let matters sit.

Let's now visit with Ruth and see how, following a lifetime of hurt, she achieved emotional healing by reshaping her thinking and behaviour.

Ruth's Story

Ruth, a thirty-seven-year-old secondary school teacher, attends Dr Jim with a long history of personal-relationship difficulties, where she struggles with any form of serious commitment. She admits to being suspicious and hypersensitive in relationships, but is struggling to understand the reasons for this. She wonders if it might be due to a long history of emotional difficulties with her mum, who is still alive. Her father passed away in his early sixties from bowel cancer, two years earlier.

Discussion reveals that she had always believed her mum prioritised her three siblings over her, which may explain her perceived negative treatment of her as a child and adolescent. 'It continues to this day,' she adds. 'Mum never wants to know anything about my life but is quick to share how well the others are doing.'

Dr Jim empathizes with her difficulties and offers to assist her to look at these issues by using some CBT techniques. He explains about rational and irrational beliefs and lays out the ABC concepts, explaining how they will employ this system to locate and manage her irrational beliefs. They decide to use her mother's treatment of her as a child as the trigger.

'How did this make you feel emotionally?' asks Dr Jim.

Ruth admits to being 'hopeless' at identifying her emotions. To assist, Dr Jim gives her the Emotional Menu which acts as a prompt. She decides that her main emotion was hurt, regularly followed by the emotion of depression.

'What was your behavioural response to your emotion of hurt?' asks Dr Jim. 'What did you do when you felt like this?'

Ruth admits to building a wall around herself, to ensure that nobody else would hurt her, and to becoming hypersensitive if anyone was in any way critical of her.

'I know people are walking on eggshells around me,' she admits, 'but I am determined that nobody will ever again treat me like my mother has for decades.'

Ruth adds that, as a result of holding this grudge, she is extremely short-fused with her mum and siblings, which has led to more than one family row.

She also admits to behaving similarly in her personal relationships, with few men able to sustain her constant suspicion and hypersensitivity to any form of comment or criticism, however well-intentioned such might be. This was ending up with her feeling increasingly alone, lonely and bitter. Her colleagues at work were also wary, giving her a wide berth in the staff room.

'And what was your behaviour when experiencing the emotion of depression?' asks Dr Jim.

Ruth admits to withdrawing socially and ruminating constantly as to how weak she was, and on occasions to drinking too much wine, which only made her feel worse.

'And how did these emotions impact on you physically?' Dr Jim asks. Ruth admits to years of fatigue, feeling constantly on edge, experiencing tension headaches and, on occasion, concentration difficulties.

They add this information to Ruth's ABC:

A – Activating Event:
- Trigger: mother's negative treatment of her as a child
- Inference/danger:

B – Belief/Demands:

C – Consequences:
- Emotional reactions: hurt and depression
- Physical reactions: fatigue; tension headaches; poor concentration; constantly on edge
- Behaviour: hiding behind a defensive wall which she places around herself; short-fused with family members, especially her mother and siblings; hypersensitive with friends and work colleagues to any form of criticism; unable to hold down personal relationships for the same reason; constant rumination on how weak she is; withdraws socially on occasions; imbibes more wine than usual.

Dr Jim then explores what inferences she had taken from her mum's treatment of her as a child that led her to experience emotions of hurt and depression. He begins by asking Ruth, 'What was it about the way that your mother treated you as a child that caused you to feel hurt?'

'Because it was so unfair,' Ruth replies. 'I know that she resented me from the beginning, as my dad simply worshipped the ground I stood on, as I was the youngest. I am not sure if this explains why she behaved towards me the way she did.'

'But in what way did she treat you unfairly?' asks Dr Jim.

'She always sided with my siblings if there was a row, for starters,' explains Ruth. 'She would constantly praise their efforts, whilst ignoring anything that I did, no matter how much I tried to earn her affection. My dad tried everything he could to make up for her treatment of me, as he sensed that I was getting the short end of the stick, but this just made matters worse.'

'Anything else?' queries Dr Jim.

There was a moment of silence. Then Ruth looks away and whispers, 'She didn't protect me!'

Dr Jim is puzzled by this comment. 'Protect you from what?'

'When I was in my early teens,' she explains, 'her brother used to visit us every few months. On five or six occasions, he touched me inappropriately, which I found distressing. On several occasions, my mum was in the house at the time, and must have known what was going on, but never intervened or tried to stop him. It came to a head when I was just fifteen, when he tried to go further, but I managed to push him away and threatened to tell my dad. He never came near me after that.'

'Did you inform anyone at the time?' asks Dr Jim. 'Either your parents or any other adult?'

Ruth looks down. 'I felt ashamed at the time,' she answers. 'I also felt that my mum would not have believed me and would have taken the side of her brother. I also knew that it would upset my dad and didn't want that, so I kept it to myself. You are the first person that I have told this to.' She adds, with tears in her eyes, 'It feels so good to have got it out on the table after all these years.'

Dr Jim agrees and suggests that this might be one of the primary reasons behind her hurt and indeed her emotion of depression. On further probing, Ruth reveals that her uncle was now deceased, but that the damage inflicted upon her remains, as she found it difficult to trust anyone, especially men. Dr Jim promises to return to this subject later. He then asks, 'What was it about the way that your mother treated you as a child that caused you to feel depressed?'

'I was so weak and useless at being unable to stand up to her. I still feel like this if I believe that I have allowed others to treat me unfairly. Only "weak people" allow others to walk over them like this!'

'And what was it about your uncle's behaviour that made you depressed?' Dr Jim asks. Ruth replies that following the encounters with her uncle, she had come to believe that she was worthless, unlovable and abnormal. At times she admitted that she almost felt responsible for what happened.

Dr Jim empathizes with her. He then suggests that they might examine what irrational beliefs were triggered by this situation and the inferences assigned to it. 'This usually takes the form of some absolute demands you were making about the trigger, which in this case was how your mother treated you,' he adds.

With Dr Jim's assistance, Ruth decides that her belief in relation to her emotion of hurt was 'that she should have been treated fairly'. Her belief in relation to her emotion of depression was 'because she had allowed her mum and others to treat her in such a manner, she was a failure and weak'. They also agree that because of her uncle's sexual advances that she also believed 'that she was worthless, abnormal and unlovable'.

They add this information to complete Ruth's ABC:

A – Activating Event:
- Trigger: mother's negative treatment of her as a child
- Inference/danger: that my mother had treated me differently to other siblings by favouring them and ig-

noring me; my mother had never praised me for positive contributions; my mother seemed to be jealous of my father's close relationship with me; she failed to protect me from the predatory advances of my uncle, who was her brother; as a consequence of my sexual abuse, I am worthless, abnormal and unlovable.

B – Belief/Demands:

- 'My mother should have treated me fairly.' 'She should have protected me from the sexual advances of my uncle.' 'I should be treated fairly.' 'Life should treat me fairly.' 'Because of my uncle's unsolicited sexual advances, I am worthless, abnormal and unlovable.'

C – Consequences:

- Emotional reactions: hurt and depression
- Physical reactions: fatigue; tension headaches; poor concentration; constantly on edge
- Behaviour: hiding behind a defensive wall which she places around herself; short-fused with family members, especially her mother and siblings; hypersensitive with friends and work colleagues to any form of criticism; unable to hold down personal relationships for the same reason; constant rumination on how weak she is; withdraws socially on occasions; more wine than usual.

Now Ruth had a clearer picture of why her whole life had been so disrupted and filled with emotional pain and distress. She was now ready to work with Dr Jim to deconstruct her emotional distress.

He begins by challenging her behaviour. How could hiding behind defensive walls, being short-fused with family, friends and work colleagues, or pushing away potential male friends, withdrawing socially or excessive alcohol be of assistance in dealing with her hurt? Ruth agrees and vows to make significant changes, with his assistance, to her life.

Dr Jim then challenges Ruth's irrational beliefs and demands. They begin with her belief that because of her uncle's sexual advances, she is worthless, abnormal and unlovable.

'Is this a rational or irrational belief?' he asks.

Ruth is silent for some time and then replies, 'To me, it seems rational as it is what I have always believed about myself, since my teens. And that because of what he did that I am now tainted, not normal like everyone else, and above all unlovable.'

Dr Jim disagrees, 'Ruth, this is a completely irrational belief.'

To persuade her of this truth, Dr Jim then asks her to perform the Rating Exercise, which challenges Ruth's perceptions. For the first time in her life, she comes to understand that human beings cannot be rated or measured in such a manner, but that their actions and behaviour could. She now sees how she had been merging who she was as a person with her behaviour, which she now realizes included her skills, attributes and talents. This led to a long discussion on the role of her inner pathological critic, how it had been formed and informed by her sexual abuse by her uncle, how it was the source of her belief that she was worthless, ugly and abnormal. Ruth admits to Dr Jim how this bullying voice had been running and destroying her life since she was a teenager. He promises to show her how to put the bully back in its box.

Dr Jim then introduces her to the world of Unconditional Self-Acceptance, where she would become comfortable in her own skin by learning to accept herself as the special unique human being that she is. To achieve this, she would have to cease rating or judging herself or allowing others to do so, but would be free to rate and take responsibility for her behaviour.

He asks her to perform the Unconditional Self-Acceptance

Exercise, mentioned in previous chapters, for the next three months. Ruth, intrigued by the concept of being comfortable in her own skin, readily agrees to put it into practice, whilst accepting that it will be challenging.

Dr Jim then disputes her demand that 'she must be treated fairly and that others, including her mother, must treat her fairly.'

'Is this a rational or irrational belief?' he asks.

Ruth initially argues that it is a completely rational and sensible demand.

'Why should I not be treated fairly?' she protests. 'Is this not a basic human right? Surely it is also not too much to ask that my own mother should treat me fairly?'

Dr Jim explains that many of his patients believe they should be treated fairly, but in real life this is a completely irrational and impossible-to-achieve demand.

Ruth is stunned by this statement.

'Are you saying that I should not be treated fairly by others?' she says indignantly. 'Is this not letting everyone else off the hook?'

Dr Jim disagrees and promises to demonstrate to her later how others would not be let off the hook in relation to their behaviour. But his first job is to persuade her that whilst it is rational to prefer that others and life should treat us fairly, in the real world this is an unrealistic and unachievable demand. On reflection, Ruth begins to see that Dr Jim is probably correct.

Dr Jim then explains that hurt is all about the 'grudge'. Ruth is intrigued by this statement and asks him to clarify further.

'If you are hurt by someone or by life,' he elaborates, 'you are carrying a grudge against that person.'

This leads to a discussion on how Ruth was carrying a grudge against her mum and siblings, how this grudge was damaging her mental health and how the only person the grudge was hurting was herself. They also discuss how easy it was to pass this grudge on to other people who cross our path, by our irritable or aggressive or sullen behaviour. He then gives Ruth the Rucksack of Rocks Exercise described earlier to carry out at home, to demonstrate how heavy a load she was carrying, and what relief she would feel to drop the grudge.

'But how do I drop this load?' she asks.

Dr Jim then returns to their conversation on Unconditional Self-Acceptance and how she was not allowed to rate herself as a person but could rate and challenge her actions or behaviour.

'Do you now see that this is the basis of your mental health?' he asks, and Ruth accepts that it is.

This leads to a fruitful discussion on how we all mess up in relation to our behaviour or actions. Dr Jim notes wryly that he too messed up regularly in his everyday life, but as long as he was trying to do his best, he accepts this as part of being a normal human being. This was a light-bulb moment for Ruth as she begins to quickly connect all the dots in her head.

'What you are saying is that we cannot rate or judge ourselves as human beings,' she says, 'but we are entitled to challenge our behaviour. Since none of us are perfect, however, we must accept that we will regularly mess up. Not only that, you are asking me to see my mum and siblings in the same light?'

Dr Jim agrees. 'Your mum and the others are normal human beings like us. They therefore cannot be rated or measured as persons just as we cannot rate ourselves. However, you are certainly free to rate and challenge their behaviour.'

Ruth now understands. 'What you are suggesting is that I forgive my mum and my siblings, not because it helps them, but because it helps me. But that I am free to speak to them about their behaviour if I deem it to be inappropriate?'

'This is how you drop a grudge,' says Dr Jim. 'You forgive the person but challenge their behaviour if deemed to be an issue.'

'But how do I challenge a person's behaviour?' asks Ruth.

What follows is an interesting discussion, where Dr Jim lays out the steps already discussed earlier in this chapter, as to how best to challenge a person's behaviour. What stands out for Ruth is the importance of intervening 'immediately' when someone hurts her through their behaviour or actions, and challenging the person directly as soon as possible. She now understands that spending days at home ruminating and becoming increasingly bitter and hostile was counterproductive and only harming herself.

They also discuss the importance of only using the 'nuclear option' when all other approaches have failed and if it were felt to be in Ruth's best interests to do so. Ruth understood that she now had choices and could decide whether or not to challenge a person's behaviour, or to make them feel the consequences of their actions.

Applying these principles to her mum's situation, Ruth realizes that she is able to forgive her as a person and continue to love her as her mother, but is looking forward to having a clear and frank conversation with her on past and present actions, which she deemed unacceptable.

The next few months are life-changing for Ruth as she battles initially with her internal pathological critic via the Unconditional Self-Acceptance Exercise. She fills several diaries with her arguments with the monster residing within her emotional brain. But slowly and gradually, the butterfly emerges, the restrictive cocoon is cast aside as she accepts herself for the special, unique and beautiful person she is. As she explains to Dr Jim on subsequent visits, she no longer believes the nonsense that she is worthless or unlovable but is becoming increasingly comfortable in her own skin. This has led to her emotion of depression becoming a fading memory.

She sits down with her mum for what would turn out to be an emotional and life-altering conversation for both. Her mum is upset on discovering how her behaviour over the years had caused Ruth so much distress. She reveals how she had suffered a bout of severe post-natal depression following Ruth's birth and had struggled to bond with her as a result. She also admits that it had caused friction between her husband and herself and that she had been jealous of how her husband had doted on Ruth, whilst not supporting her during her bout of depression.

Her mum cries uncontrollably on being informed by Ruth that her uncle had attempted to sexually abuse her. She genuinely had never noticed what had been going on, and was not in a good place herself at the time. She is shocked and hurt that the brother she trusted would have tried to molest her own daughter. Ruth ends up trying to console her mum with a loving embrace, which breaks down years of underlying hurt, confusion and emotional pain for both.

This conversation finishes with both agreeing to work hard at repairing all the years of hurt and to emotionally nourish and care for each other.

Ruth has similar conversations with her siblings, who are equally devastated and upset for her and who promise to change their behaviours towards her. She also works hard in her work situation, to stop carrying grudges and develop with Dr Jim's assistance – her sense of humour, to stop taking small things too seriously and instead dismiss them with an appropriate quip. Her work environment becomes an increasingly pleasant one because of her changed behaviour.

But the real benefits come in her personal relationships with men as she now, with Dr Jim's assistance (and some counselling in relation to her abuse as suggested by him), comes to the realisation that she has to learn to trust again in this area. She accepts that some men's behaviour could be inappropriate and should be challenged quickly and firmly, but that most men are genuine and deserve to be given her the benefit of the doubt. This has allowed Ruth to re-enter the dating scene, where she is gradually learning to trust again, and she feels it is only a matter of time before she meets 'Mr Right'. As Ruth shares with Dr Jim, by dropping her grudges and hurts and learning to trust again, she has found a new relationship with her mum, siblings and is at last free to explore future relationships, free of suspicion and hurt.

Key Learning Points
1. Hurt is one of the most toxic, self-destructive, unhealthy negative emotions of all, often triggered by a perception that you are being treated unfairly by others or life. It burns everything it comes in contact with and can easily turn your life into an arid desert. It can also grow legs, so you will increasingly carry your hurt into future relationships and situations and impose it on others.
2. Underlying hurt is the irrational belief that you should be treated fairly or that life should treat you fairly.
3. To manage hurt, you must begin to confront and challenge your irrational beliefs and demands and change the unhealthy behavioural patterns which ensue.
4. To challenge your thinking, you must accept that hurt is about holding a grudge against a person, organization or indeed life itself. You must acknowledge that holding this grudge is simply harming yourself and not affecting those who have caused the hurt. To drop the grudge, you must

learn to forgive the person who has caused the hurt, but feel free to challenge their behaviour. This will require you to use the Turtle Exercise to calm down (see page 135) and then immediately challenge the person's behaviour and make them understand how this has affected you. On rare occasions you may use the nuclear option and ban the person from your life altogether.

5. It is also important to confront and challenge your negative behavioural patterns which have arisen, secondary to your hurt.

7. Anger

Would you like to know what to do when the 'red mists' descend and you find yourself embroiled in angry confrontations with others? How to temper and manage those anger outbursts, which are causing both yourself and others emotional distress? Would you like to become a calmer, more peaceful person, slow to anger and less likely to suffer the negative consequences which can result from such outbursts? If so, read on.

What is Anger?

Anger (and its sidekick, rage), for the purposes of our discussion, is an unhealthy negative emotion, which is triggered by the belief that someone has wronged us and should be punished accordingly. From an evolutionary perspective, anger, together with fear and anxiety, were important emotions that were essential for our survival. The latter assisted us to run if there was danger, whilst the former prepared us to get into battle mode, to engage with whatever was perceived as a threat to our survival. In both cases, these emotions strongly activated our internal stress systems, as explored in chapter one. If fearful, we pour out adrenaline, which prepares us to run. If angry, we pump out our aggression hormone noradrenaline, plus glucocortisol, our chronic stress hormone, and in some cases, our sex hormone, testosterone. It is these hormones, especially noradrenaline and glucocortisol, that give rise to most of the physical consequences of anger, which we will explore later. The role of testosterone in anger is less clear. Traditionally it has been assumed that, since men seemed to be on the surface displaying greater levels of anger, it must act by increasing levels of aggression. Its role is now felt to be less associated with aggression and more to do with claiming dominance or power over others.

There are two common types of anger, and you may recognise yourself in one of these descriptions:

1. Passive Aggressive – Here you may find yourself internalising your anger, with levels building up inside like a pressure cooker, ready to explode. Because you are someone who dislikes confrontation, you suppress your anger, becoming sullen, cold, irritable, prone to procrastination, moody and difficult to live with, as you may be taking your unexpressed anger out on those close to you, without them understanding the reasons for your behaviour.

2. Openly Aggressive – This is where your anger is easily and rapidly externalised in the form of verbal or physical aggressive behaviour. It descends into rage when you completely lose control of your emotions and behaviour. This latter behaviour can be extremely destructive and is seen in fighting, bullying, road-rage incidents and domestic abuse. It can also lead to regular interactions with the law, if allowed to run unchecked. Some may notice that alcohol fuels and releases this form of anger.

It is useful to recognise some of the physical symptoms which anger can engender in us. You may notice that your heart rate accelerates, your breathing becomes faster, your face becomes flushed, your hands clench and your facial and other muscles tighten up. The purpose of these changes is to prepare your body to physically fight.

Frequent anger comes with consequences to the body. If constantly exposed to this emotion, we can experience increased risks of high blood pressure, strokes, heart attacks and cardiac arrythmias. From a mental-health perspective, anger is often associated with increased risks of clinical depression, self-harm and suicide, alcohol and substance abuse and psychopathy. From a personal and social perspective, anger is associated with relationship difficulties and separations, and work conflicts, and escalates all the way up to coercive control, domestic abuse, road rage, violence against others, conflict with authorities and in rare cases even homicide.

There can be little doubt that some of us are more prone from a genetic and family-history perspective to develop this emotion. Environment, too, plays a major role, with childhood and adolescent experiences shaping the beliefs which can trigger anger.

In my experience, the majority of those who struggle with the emotion of anger do not seek help. This makes sense as they perceive 'others' as the problem and not themselves. Doctors and therapists, unfortunately, are more likely to be assisting those who are at the receiving end of this emotion.

Some confuse anger with other negative emotions such as hurt and frustration. Many people who believe they are struggling with anger are surprised to discover that the real culprit is hurt. This occurs as there are commonalities between both emotions. As we saw in the previous chapter, when hurt we may believe that we are not being treated fairly. Anger is more about punishing those who have, in our minds, wronged us.

Anger can be equally confused with the emotion of frustration. Frustration is an extremely common unhealthy negative emotion, whereby we believe that the changes which we want to see in the world should come from others and not from ourselves. When frustrated, we often feel that other people need to change, rather than recognising that the power to change often rests with ourselves. Because some of the behaviours relating to anger and frustration can be similar, such as irritability, or verbally or aggressive behaviour on the road, some mistake the two emotions. Because there can also be similar (if lesser) physical consequences to frustration, this confusion is understandable. In my experience, anger is a more destructive emotion to ourselves and those we love.

There is a cultural perspective that men are more likely than women to experience and display the emotion of anger. What little research exists suggests otherwise – there is little gender difference in the experience of anger, though there is some difference in how that anger is expressed by men and women.

In relation to potential triggers, when you are prone to anger, almost anything can set you off. Relationships, both personal and familial, are a major flashpoint, as are areas such as the workplace, sporting arenas, neighbours, drinking sessions, road rage and so on. The reality for the person who struggles with this emotion is that they often don't have to seek out trouble, it invariably finds them.

Finally, anger can regularly be linked with other unhealthy negative emotions. Fear and anger can occur together, as can depression and anger, frustration and anger and occasionally hurt and anger. The most lethal combination is pathological jealousy and anger, which can in serious cases lead to domestic abuse, homicide or murder-suicide.

How to Manage the Emotion of Anger

If you can relate to the above and find yourself struggling with anger issues, it is critical to explore what underlies this emotion, and how best to manage it. At the heart of the emotion of anger lies the belief that someone has wronged us and, because they have, they are bad and must be punished for it. On occasions, the anger may be self-directed, where the belief might be because I have done something that I should not have, I am bad and must be punished. While this might seem to be perfectly rational to the angry person, and provides an excuse to lash out verbally, physically or emotionally, the reality is that this is an irrational, destructive belief. There are two parts to this belief which are irrational and unhealthy. The first is a belief that human beings can be rated or measured as bad. This is of course another form of personal rating, which as we have already explored is flawed, as human beings cannot be rated, only our behaviour. If we believe that someone has wronged us, it is their behaviour which is 'bad' or inappropriate, not the person themselves.

The second is the absolute demand that the person must be punished. Is this rational or sensible? The consequences for both you, the 'punisher', and the person you punish may be significant. Would it not be healthier and more rational to deal with the person who has supposedly wronged us calmly and appropriately?

You must further consider whether your natural responses to anger, such as physical violence, verbal abuse, passive-aggressive behaviour, etc., are damaging you more than the person you wish to punish. If you are struggling to accept this reality, then consider answering one question, when you have cooled off from the immediate sensation of anger: 'Is my behaviour helping or damaging me in my life?' Invariably, if you are being honest with yourself, the answer will be that it is causing you harm. Just consider the stream of negative consequences following some such aggressive behaviours. These may take the form of strained or broken relationships, constant conflict and fights, trouble with the law, work difficulties and so on. Is this the way you wish to live your life?

There will be some reading this chapter who will not wish to change their thinking or behaviour, and who insist that they are justified in their anger and the behaviour that stems from it. Remember that, as human beings, we only change our behaviour when the cost gets too high, and for some with anger issues this can involve quite a wait. But change is possible with effort.

If you do wish to challenge and change your irrational beliefs and unhealthy behaviours and learn how to banish anger from your life, then here are several suggestions:

1. Consider attending anger-management courses, run by trained professionals.
2. Try to be honest in admitting that you have a problem and that your emotion and behaviour are impacting severely on the lives of those around you. If you don't think your anger is having an impact on others, ask them if they agree with you on this.
3. Focus initially on your behaviour, which is usually self-destructive. Learn the Turtle Exercise (see page 135), where you must withdraw for five to ten minutes till the initial emotion has calmed down. Only then should you try to rationally problem-solve the issue with the person or institution involved, which of course is the short cut to dealing with your anger difficulties. Avoid alcohol or obvious triggering situations, which you know will often lead to angry outbursts.

4. Try initially to develop Unconditional Self-Acceptance, where you learn to cease personally rating or measuring both yourself or other human beings but focus instead on rating both your own behaviour and that of the person you believe has wronged you. This shifts the focus of your thinking on to their behaviour or actions, rather than personalising it.

5. Try to develop an understanding of what seems to set you off and then build in some protective barriers to avoid or deal better with such triggering situations or events.

6. The single most important message, following the Turtle Exercise, is to write down the circumstances which have triggered your emotion of anger and identify the irrational belief and unhealthy behaviours underlying it. Later, we will see how Matthew learned to do this as part of his journey towards emotional healing.

7. Lastly, remember that there will be a high cost to not dealing with your anger, both to yourself and those who love you. No matter how difficult it can be to challenge your thinking and actively change your behaviour, it pales into insignificance when compared with the devastation that may follow if you don't.

Let's now meet Matthew and see how he turns his life around by taking the above steps and putting them into action.

Matthew's Story

Matthew, a thirty-eight-year-old, high-powered company executive, reluctantly agrees to attend Dr Jim, at the express request of both his company and partner, Maura. He has always suffered from anger issues. His mother gently remarked to him on one occasion that he was 'born angry' as he had a temper from the beginning. She also remarked how alike he was to his father, who had struggled with anger issues his whole life, unfortunately dying early from a stroke when Matthew was sixteen. His mother always believed that his stroke was a direct result of these anger issues and she, too, encouraged Matthew to seek assistance. This process is accelerated when he attends his family doctor and discovers his blood pressure is beginning to rise – and the possibility of medication for life beckons. None of this, however, makes the slightest difference to how annoyed and upset Matthew is at having to attend Dr Jim in the first place.

'If the truth be told,' he tells Dr Jim, 'I am so angry that I have to come here at all. If everyone else would mind their own business and let me get on with my life, everything would be fine!'

'If that is the case,' asks Dr Jim, 'then why are you here at all? I certainly do not wish to waste your time or mine.'

'I am not getting at you,' Matthew replies. 'It's just that I am upset that my company and my partner, not to mention my mother, are all on my back and believe that I have anger issues!'

'Do you believe that they are all wrong?' asks Dr Jim innocently.

This stops Matthew in his tracks, as he is forced to reflect on whether this statement is true or false.

'Well, maybe I do lose my cool sometimes,' he admits. 'But am I not entitled to do so, if people, in my opinion, are in the wrong?'

'And is losing your cool helping you in your life at present?' asks Dr Jim.

On reflection, Matthew admits that his anger outbursts are getting him into trouble with work colleagues and at home with Maura.

'Maybe I do need to explore some techniques to keep my anger at bay,' he says, 'but I am not sure if I can change. I am so like my dad. I harbour it all inside for ages and then just blow.'

Dr Jim empathises and agrees that confronting anger is one of the most difficult challenges that any of us can take on, but he is prepared to work with Matthew on two conditions. The first is that Matthew must accept that he does have anger issues. The second is that he accepts that it is not only in Matthew's interest to challenge his anger, but in the interests of Maura, his mother and his work colleagues.

With some reluctance, Matthew accepts these conditions, and accepts that Dr Jim is not 'the enemy' but rather someone who might perhaps assist him to make changes in his life, which would benefit all.

Dr Jim offers to assist him in managing his anger issues, using some CBT techniques. He explains about rational and irrational beliefs and lays out the ABC concepts, explaining how they will employ this system to locate and manage his irrational beliefs. They decide to use the example of a recent work situation where his boss accused him, unfairly in Matthew's mind, of losing an important client, by being short with him on the phone.

'And how did this make you feel emotionally?' asks Dr Jim.

'I was so angry,' he replies. 'Fuming internally and struggling to keep a lid on it.'

'Any other emotions?' asks Dr Jim.

'I also felt frustrated' he replies, 'and later depressed for letting him get away with it.'

'How did your emotion of anger make you feel physically?' asks Dr Jim.

Matthew admits to spending hours with his heart pounding, muscles clenched, cheeks burning and eventually he developed a splitting tension headache. 'I was tensed up like a wound-up drum, with my body feeling as if it was completely stretched to breaking point.'

'What was your behavioural response to these emotions?' asks Dr Jim. 'What did you do when you felt like this?'

Matthew reveals a litany of unhealthy behaviours, where he went into a sullen silence, avoided direct confrontation with his boss but instead harboured a deep resentment, becoming moody and sullen with work colleagues, ruminating constantly for the rest of the week, becoming moody, sulky and distant with Maura, snapping at her for the smallest of issues and hitting the bottle, which only increased his inner anger. He also admits to picking up some penalty points for speeding and getting into a road-rage incident with a motorist on his way home the following day. 'I was trying to release the anger out of my system,' he admits, 'but that didn't work out so well!'

They add this information to Matthew's ABC:

A – Activating Event:
- Trigger: accusation by boss that Matthew had lost a valuable client
- Inference/danger:

B – Belief/Demands:

C – Consequences:
- Emotional reactions: anger, frustration and depression
- Behaviour: descends into sullen silence; moody with work colleagues; avoids confrontation with boss but harbours resentment; ruminates constantly; moody and bad-tempered with Maura; speeding fines and road-rage incident; excessive alcohol consumption.

Dr Jim then asks, 'What was it about your boss's accusation that you had lost the firm a valuable client which caused you feel angry?'

'Because he was obviously wrong,' answers Matthew, who can already feel himself becoming physically tense, just recalling the incident.

'Why, in your opinion, was he wrong?' queries Dr Jim.

'The client in question was a pain in the neck, from the beginning,' explains Matthew. 'He was always argumentative and demanding and trying to stir up trouble. It was inevitable that he was going to leave, somewhere down the line. The fact that it was me that happened to answer the phone that day, was in my mind incidental.'

'Anything else?' asks Dr Jim.

'My boss picked on me in front of everyone, making me look stupid and inept, which of course I am not,' he replies. 'He was clearly in the wrong, but didn't even apologise later. He deserves to be punished in some way for his actions.'

'And what was it about his comments that made you feel frustrated?' asks Dr Jim.

Matthew replies, 'If only the boss, and indeed the client, could see things as clearly as I do. If they did, I could have avoided the discomfort and hassle of the following days.'

'And depression?' asks Dr Jim. 'Why did you feel that afterwards?'

'Only weak people allow others, such as the boss, to push them around,' replies Matthew. 'I felt that I was a failure for not standing up to him and letting him know how wrong he was.'

'Let's examine what irrational beliefs were triggered by your boss's negative comments, and the inferences you assigned to it,' says Dr Jim. 'This usually takes the form of some absolute demands you were making about the trigger, which in this case was his suggestion that you were responsible for losing a client.'

Following discussion, Matthew agrees that his belief underlying his anger was that his boss should not have done what he did to him, and that because he did, he should be punished. In relation to his emotion of depression, it was that because he had allowed his boss to treat him like this, Matthew was weak and a failure. Underlying his emotion of frustration lay the irrational belief that others, such as the client and his boss, should make changes but that he himself was not obliged to do so, and that he should not have to put up with discomfort.

They add this information to complete Matthew's ABC:

A – Activating Event:
- Trigger: accusation by boss that Matthew had lost a valuable client
- Inference/danger: my boss was wrong to ascribe the client leaving to my management, as the client was argumentative and awkward and was going to leave anyway; my boss was wrong to make a show of me in front of other colleagues; my boss deserved to be punished for his actions; that I was weak and a failure for allowing my boss to treat me like this; if only the boss and the client could see things as clearly as I did, I would not have had to endure the discomfort of the days following the incident.

B – Belief/Demands:
- 'The boss should not have done that to me, but because he did, he is bad and should be punished.' 'Because I allowed him to treat me this way, I am weak and a failure.' 'The client, my boss and the world in general must change to suit me.' 'I should not have to suffer any discomfort.'

C – Consequences:
- Emotional reactions: anger, depression and frustration
- Behaviour: descends into sullen silence; moody with

work colleagues; avoids confrontation with boss but harbours resentment; ruminating constantly; moody and
bad-tempered with Maura; speeding fines and road-rage
incident; excessive alcohol consumption.

Matthew now has a clearer picture of why he had become so distressed by what had occurred.

'This incident is a microcosm of what happens to me on a daily
and weekly basis,' he admits, 'but how can I change this pattern?'

Dr Jim explains that change is possible, with plenty of engage-
ment and hard work to change the irrational beliefs and unhealthy
behaviours which have blighted Matthew's life to date.

They begin by challenging Matthew's unhealthy behaviours.
They agree that harbouring resentments, avoiding confrontation,
being moody and bad-tempered with his partner, boss and work
colleagues, drinking excessively and becoming involved in road
rage or speeding were simply adding to his woes. Matthew promises to work with Dr Jim to challenge and change his actions.

They then explore his belief in relation to his boss that 'he
should not have done what he did to Matthew, but because he did,
he is bad and should be punished'.

'Is this a rational or irrational belief?' Dr Jim asks.

'Of course it is rational,' protests Matthew. 'He shouldn't have
wronged me the way he did. Certainly, in my mind he is bad and
should be punished for his actions.'

This leads to a heated discussion on whether this is a sensible
rational belief which would help Matthew in his life, or an irrational one, that would cause him long-term difficulties if he insists
on holding on to it.

'But what other way is there to understand what happened?'
asks Matthew.

'We will explore this later,' replies Dr Jim, 'but firstly, I would like to divert to your belief that because you allowed him to treat you this way, you are weak and a failure. It was this belief that led you to experience the emotion of depression. Is this belief rational or irrational?'

Once again, Matthew struggles to accept that it is an irrational belief.

'Am I not weak and a failure by not putting my boss in his place instead of allowing him to walk all over me, in front of others?'

'But can a human being be measured or discussed in such terms?' asks Dr Jim.

When Matthew continues to struggle, Dr Jim asks him to carry out the Rating Exercise where he rates himself at ninety out of a hundred and believes others would apply a similar rating. When asked where he rated himself when put down by his boss, he drops his rating to eighty, with a gesture of disgust, and suggested that others would do likewise.

'But on what grounds were you rating yourself as a human being?' asks Dr Jim. Matthew, for once, is stumped for a reply, but admits on reflection that the only thing that human beings can be rated on is their behaviour or talents. Dr Jim agrees and elaborates further. 'We all play the rating game, merging who we are personally as individual beings with our behaviour and other attributes. If successful with the latter, we rate ourselves upwards; if not, then downwards. This is a process designed to make us miserable.'

Matthew could relate to this process, as he did indeed expect high standards of himself and struggled when unable to achieve them.

This leads to a discussion on how all of us have an internal critic which Dr Jim calls the 'pathological critic'. 'This is the voice in your head, which is so self-critical of everything we say and do.'

He explains further, 'It is the voice which makes you believe that you are weak or a failure, for example.'

Once again, Matthew could relate to this voice, which regularly mocked him if he was not achieving the high bar which he set for himself.

Dr Jim then introduces Matthew to the world of Unconditional Self-Acceptance, where he would become comfortable in his own skin by learning to accept himself as the special unique human being that he is. To achieve this, he would have to cease rating or judging himself or allowing others to do so but would be free to rate and take responsibility for his behaviour. He asks him to perform the Unconditional Self-Acceptance Exercise, mentioned earlier, for the next few months.

Matthew is intrigued by the concept which is so foreign to him. It feels as if he is letting himself off the hook too easily! He mentions this to Dr Jim, who replies: 'It is the opposite, Matthew, for it is harder than you might think to accept responsibility for, or challenge and change your behaviour. But remember that, in life, you can only do your best in relation to your behaviour. No matter how hard you try, you are destined to mess up regularly in relation to it, as you have already discovered.'

Matthew was beginning to see the light. 'What you are trying to get me to understand is that all of us as human beings cannot be rated or "boxed" as we are too special and unique. But we have a responsibility to do our best in relation to our behaviour, whilst accepting that as human beings, we will all mess up. But if we have been trying our best, then we must learn to be kinder to ourselves?'

Dr Jim agrees and then asks, 'Can you apply this concept to the situation with your boss?'

Suddenly Matthew sees the light. 'I understand that my boss, too, is a human being, as indeed was the client, so based on our discussion, I am not allowed to rate them personally but am free to rate and challenge their behaviour.'

They also agree that, for the same reasons, his boss should never be rated as 'bad' as a person: only his behaviour could be construed as such.

This leads to a fruitful discussion on how Matthew could have handled the situation differently, with this new understanding under his belt. He could have used the Turtle Exercise and excused himself for five to ten minutes to calm down; perhaps jotted down a few thoughts on paper to engage the rational side of his brain. He could then have a firm but quiet chat with his boss, to try to give his side of the story, which might have solved the problem to begin with. It would also have meant that he did not arrive home in the passive-aggressive manner in which he did, and might also have avoided the penalty points on his driving licence. As they both agreed, it would have been in his interests to have adopted this approach, as both his working and domestic life would have benefited.

They also agree that Matthew's demand, underlying his emotion of frustration that his boss, client and the world should change to suit him was irrational. As Dr Jim jokes, 'Good luck with that one, Matthew!'

He gives him some exercises to challenge this demand, which was all about seeking long-term gain but wishing to avoid short-term pain. These exercises involved writing down his long-term goals, what short-term pain he was trying to avoid and what changes he was going to have to make to achieve his goals.

For the following six to twelve months, Matthew is challenged to the core of his being. Anger was so engrained in his psyche that it took a long period of determined hard work on his behaviours, especially, to overcome this emotion. This process was assisted by anger-management classes, suggested by Dr Jim, which taught him to identify and sidestep potential triggering situations. Luckily, he has embraced the concept of Unconditional Self-Acceptance with Maura's assistance and no longer berates himself if, on occasion, he reverts to losing it for short periods. He gradually learns to apply the Turtle Exercise on a regular basis and finds that he is subtly shifting more into 'problem-solving' mode than ruminating constantly and berating others. He has also developed a sense of humour about himself and life, which he now accepts is not going to change any time soon. Physically, his blood pressure begins to stabilise without medication, and his tension headaches decrease.

A year later, he is more at peace with himself and begins to reap the rewards of his hard work. Maura now agrees to marry him and to try for a family. His boss, delighted with the changes which Matthew has brought about in himself, rewards him with a promotion. His relationship with his mum also improves.

Matthew and Dr Jim are glad to agree that Matthew was not doomed to follow in his father's footsteps but could instead create his own destiny. Dr Jim describes the process as 'emotional healing'.

Key Learning Points

1. Anger is an extremely destructive, unhealthy negative emotion and can cause physical and psychological difficulties for both you and those who live and work with you.
2. Underlying anger is the irrational belief that others should not have wronged you the way they did, and that because they did, they are bad and must be punished for their actions.
3. It is often our unhealthy behaviours in anger that cause so much difficulty both to ourselves and those we love.

4. To deal with anger, you must learn to firstly challenge and change many of the self-destructive behaviours which manifest with this emotion. This will have benefits for both you and your loved ones. This may involve anger-management classes.

5. You will then have to challenge your irrational belief that the person(s) who have offended you must be punished. Is it in your interests to be judge, jury and executioner? Or is this belief and subsequent behaviours assisting or damaging you in your life? It is only when you accept that anger is damaging your life that you will find yourself on the road to challenging and changing it.

6. Finally, it is important to develop Unconditional Self-Acceptance, where you accept that neither you nor those you believe have wronged you can be rated as human beings, but that you can rate your behaviour and indeed theirs. Human beings, for example, are not 'bad' but their behaviours can be described and rated as such.

PART FIVE

Grief

8. Grief

Have you found yourself struggling with the world of loss and be-reavement and unsure as to where it is leading you or how to manage it? Would you like to know how long your grief might last and why you may be finding it so difficult to cope with? Are you struggling with the changes to your life that come with losing someone special to you? Would you like to come to some form of emotional healing, no matter how painful your loss has been? To find some inner peace and a pathway out of the darkness which you may be encountering at present? If the answer to any of these questions is yes, read on.

The experiences of loss and grief are universal. There are few of us who have not experienced the raw emotions that are unleashed when a loved one dies. Who has not had to face the ultimate questions about themselves and the meaning of life which death and loss bring? For grief can present the ultimate challenge to our psychological wellbeing. This section will hopefully assist you to make it through the many emotions that can threaten to over-whelm us in such situations.

I will share with you insights from countless patients who have allowed me the privilege of walking beside them on their journey of grief.

We will examine how it is possible, over time, to come to terms with your grief. We will explore how to manage the emotions unleashed by loss. We will consider the effects of change in the grieving process. We will also discuss the unhelpful ideas, beliefs, thinking patterns, emotions and behaviours which can complicate this process. And crucially, we will learn how to restructure them so that you can see a way towards emotional healing.

You may find yourself becoming extremely emotional as you explore these chapters. The stories I share may trigger deep-seated and often raw emotions and memories. But please don't be distressed by your tears; releasing these emotions is healthy and not something to be either afraid or ashamed of. It is just part of a long process of emotional healing which hopefully, by the end of this section, you may understand better.

What is Grief?

Grief can be best described as a condition where we experience intense sorrow, sadness, emotional pain or heartache, arising from the death of a loved one. The term 'grief' is often ascribed to other losses which may occur in our lives. The loss or break-up of a significant relationship, the death of a beloved pet, the loss of a job and so on. I believe that using the term in such situations, whilst technically correct, runs the risk of diminishing the particular difficulties which face those who have lost loved ones to the harsh spectre of death. I will confine myself solely therefore to its usage in this context.

This is not to say that other losses in life cannot be intensely emotionally distressing, because they can. Nor that the grief process which we are about to explore is in any way different, from, say, the break-up of a significant relationship, because in practice both situations can be similar. Nor that the process of emotional healing in relation to such a loss is any different. It is just that the death of a loved one is perhaps the greatest loss which any of us can ever experience in life. If you are grieving the loss of a personal or other important relationship, or even a much-loved pet, the information and understanding which you may garner in this section may be helpful to you.

Grief is a completely natural process and should never be seen as something abnormal. There is sometimes confusion between the terms 'grief' and 'bereavement'. The former relates to our emotional responses to the loss of a loved one. The latter, on the other hand, is seen as either the period of mourning that occurs following their death, or the process of coping with it. Some regard grief as an 'emotion' that we experience when someone close to us dies. I don't consider it useful to see it that way, as grief is not an emotion but a process which, as we will explore, can throw up a host of different emotions.

For the purposes of our discussion, I am going to use the term 'grief' to cover all aspects of what happens to us as human beings when we lose someone close to us. This process will inevitably involve the thinking, emotions, physical symptoms and behavioural consequences which a bereaved person may experience.

Grief is uniquely individual and how each one of us responds to the death of a loved one can vary substantially. It is possible, for example, for someone to encounter such a loss and not experience the emotional distress commonly felt in such situations. This emotional numbness can cause significant distress where the person in question assumes that their response is 'abnormal' and judges themselves accordingly. We will see examples of this later.

The 'Stages' of Grief

Swiss-born and American-based psychiatrist Elisabeth Kübler-Ross's seminal book *On Death and Dying* outlined the five stages experienced by the terminally ill as they came to terms with dying. From her observations of being with such patients, she described these stages as denial, anger, bargaining, depression and, finally, acceptance. She went on to suggest that the bereaved would pass through similar phases. Let's briefly summarize these five stages, detailed by Kübler-Ross, as they relate to grief.

1. Denial. This does not suggest denying that the person has actually died and is physically gone. It relates more to a sense of disbelief that the person has actually left us. We keep expecting them to walk back into the house or the phone to ring with their voice at the other end. It is usually associated with the period of numbness which follows on from their death.

2. Anger. This is seen by Kübler-Ross as being a natural progression in the grief process. Anger can be directed towards oneself, towards the loved one who has died, God, life, the medical system and so on.

3. Bargaining. This is felt to work hand in hand with guilt. We want life to be the way it was and constantly struggle with thoughts of 'if only . . .' in relation to circumstances surrounding the death of a loved one.

4. Depression. This is seen as a natural, almost automatic, emotional response to our loss. In this stage we may stop caring about ourselves and struggle with the pointlessness of everything, now that our loved one is gone.

5. Acceptance. This is seen as finally accepting the reality

that our loved one is physically gone from us and that this reality is now permanent.

Kübler-Ross's 'stages of grief' became the dominant thinking as to how the grief process should play itself out. Even today, her stages of grief are embedded in the minds of many laypeople and professionals alike.

I believe that Kübler-Ross did us all a wonderful service by trying to make sense of the raw, painful world of grief by applying the above five stages. She was trying to explore and express the reality of grief for those left behind. There will also be many who can identify themselves through these stages. However, having worked with the bereaved, especially with those who have lost long-term partners or loved ones to suicide, I have some concerns about elements of her thinking.

One would be concerned, for example, about the suggestion that grief is a 'self-limiting' condition, where you will inevitably pass through the above phases to reach a calmer, peaceful state of acceptance. This belief has led countless bereaved people to assume that they should be over their grief and, if they aren't, that there must be something abnormal about them.

A second concern would be the suggestion that every case of grief is going to be similar in relation to emotions and behaviours, and that each person passes through the above stages, with the time spent or severity of symptoms only dependent on how close they were to the person.

A final concern would be the implication that there is a 'correct' way to grieve or that human beings will proceed through the nightmare of grief in an orderly, organized manner. As someone who has walked the walk of grief, with countless wonderful people, this is rarely the case.

In her own lifetime, Kübler-Ross did engage with many of these criticisms. In her final book, *On Grief and Grieving*, which she co-wrote with David Kessler whilst dying herself, she observed that her stage theory had been misunderstood, that grief was as individual as our lives, and that the stages were not meant to be fixed on some linear timeline.

The Modern Approach to Grief

Many clinicians and psychologists have challenged the Kübler-Ross 'stages' approach to grief. One of the difficulties that faces those who question the above staged approach is the absence of an alternative agreed, scientifically validated, thought-through and widely accepted model.

There are, however, some commonly accepted modern ideas and concepts which may be of some assistance to those who are either in the throes of grief or still struggling to see light at the end of the tunnel. Let's explore some of these ideas further.

1. Every person will experience grief in a different way. Grief is as unique a process as human beings are unique.
2. Grief is a normal, human response to the loss of a loved one and should never be considered as an illness, a weakness or a disorder.
3. There is no time limit on how long each one of us will grieve for. Knowing this can be of great assistance to those still struggling with grief years after their loved one has died. A useful approach is to accept that grief takes as long as it takes. Some reading this paragraph may find this statement particularly upsetting, and wish for a quicker path out of their grief. But it is better to

face the truth, even if it seems challenging. Over time, we simply learn to cope better with managing our grief.

4. As human beings we have greater untapped resilience skills than we think. Most of us have the inner resources to cope with the pain and loss so endemic to grief without requiring professional assistance (though professional assistance can be a lifeline to those who need it).

5. We never really stop grieving over the loss of someone close to us. We just find it easier to deal with the load on our back as time passes.

6. The intensity of the grief process can vary enormously from person to person, depending on the circumstances and closeness of the relationship involved. For some, it is searing, raw and deeply painful. For others, the wound exposed may be less so.

7. It is completely normal, in some circumstances, not to experience any major negative emotional or other consequences when someone close to us dies. This is common where there has been a long period of illness, when goodbyes already have been said. Or perhaps where the relationship may be familial but not necessarily close.

8. Each person must find their own path out of grief. For some, finding this path is easier and they may find themselves coping better at an earlier stage. For others, their path may be complex, painful and takes longer. Both are completely normal and acceptable.

9. We all grieve for, and mourn after, a different person even though the same person has died. This is especially relevant if, for example, we lose a parent. It is important

to recognise that, even between siblings, everyone will mourn a different father or mother. Some members in a family may experience a stronger grief reaction than others who were not as close to the parent.

10. The symptoms of grief may be especially intense in the first six to twelve months following the death, and then gradually begin to diminish. But sometimes these symptoms may take longer to emerge or may last for considerably longer periods of time. Both are equally normal and acceptable. As we have already stated, there is no one way to grieve.

11. We sometimes use the term 'survivor' in relation to grief, especially when dealing with the death of a loved one by suicide. The reality is that in cases where the loss is felt really intensely, the best we can do for long periods is to simply survive as best we can, and wait till our own innate reserves finally assist us to cope better with the load and re-engage again with life.

The modern approach to grief is therefore more fluid and all-encompassing than Kübler-Ross's five stages. We have moved away from a fixed linear understanding of grief, where all was nicely packaged and emotionally put to bed, within a certain time-fixed frame of usually one to two years. We now see grief more as an emotional load to be carried with us on our journey through life. For some, this burden is heavier, and it may take longer to become accustomed to it. For others, the burden is lighter, and they adjust more quickly. Above all, we now understand that all of this is a normal process. It is only when we obstruct this normal process that difficulties begin to accumulate. More on this later.

The Emotional and Physical Effects of Grief

There is no one way to feel, emotionally or physically, when grieving. Some people will experience most of the emotions and physical symptoms laid out below. Others may struggle to relate to any of them. Much depends on how close we were to the deceased. For most of us, grief triggers a cascade of internal reactions, especially in the emotional memory, visual and auditory parts of the brain; and in our stress and immune systems. We will explore later the neuroscience underlying grief.

The majority of what you may feel, both in the immediate aftermath of the loss and subsequently, is emanating from these three centres (emotional, visual and auditory) and our stress and immune systems. We achieve emotional healing when most of these changes either settle or we find ourselves able to manage them better.

The Emotional Effects

Grief is a powerful emotional trigger, which can lead to completely disparate emotions from person to person. Our initial emotions may be numbed by the shock of the person dying, especially if the death is sudden or unexpected. Just because I am feeling nothing at this stage does not mean that I am not grieving or don't care. It is rather that the body's internal coping mechanisms are flooding in to give us time and space to deal with this massive trauma or blow.

I often compare this initial numbness to what happens following a knife or gunshot wound, where the initial pain is anaesthetised by the brain releasing large amounts of endorphins. These internal opiate chemicals temporarily block out the pain, but over time their effects diminish, and the pain arrives. So, too, with grief.

Here is a list of common emotions that you may experience, some of which we have explored in detail already.

1. Sadness. This is the trademark calling-card of grief. A deep-seated sadness, emanating from the core of our being. It often comes in waves, leaving us deeply distressed and on occasions triggering floods of tears. The sadness relates to the loss of someone close to us, who will not be returning. We are often mourning as much the loss of what 'might have been' if they were still alive as the person themselves.

2. Emotional Pain. You may find it strange that I am putting this in as an emotion. Over many decades of working with the bereaved, they have shared with me that grief can be associated with a deep-seated inner psychological pain. Some have described it as worse than any physical pain they have endured.

3. Guilt. I often describe this emotion as one of the 'tricksters' of grief. You may find yourself questioning many aspects of how and why your loved one died and what you could have done to prevent it. You may berate yourself that you should have spent more time with them while they were alive and so on.

4. Anger. This can be another 'trickster'. Here, we may be angry at God, at the person for dying and leaving us behind, or at the medical system for not being able to prevent the death. Or at the quality of care they received. Both guilt and anger are common emotions in grief, but they can get in the way of really experiencing the healthier emotion of sadness.

5. Anxiety. This emotion is understandable as the loss of a loved one is one of the biggest changes we will ever

encounter. We worry about how we will cope; how we will continue existing without their presence; what will become of us personally and of those left behind.

6. Depression. This emotion is often triggered when we believe that we should be coping better with our grief. That we are not over it and that there must be something abnormal about us if not.

7. Frustration. This can be triggered by how others are treating you following the loss, comments they may inadvertently make, decisions that others may thrust upon us to make, even if we are not ready to make them, and so on. This is often a missed emotion that can cause significant distress.

8. Hurt. This can be against the unfairness of life for taking your loved one away.

9. Shame. I have found this to be an intensely powerful emotion experienced especially by those who have lost a loved one to suicide, or where the person died of some condition or illness seen as socially 'less acceptable'.

There is often no seeming pattern as to when, where, how and why we may experience any of the above emotions. Each one of us, due to our unique nature, may veer into some emotional pathways more easily than others.

There is also crucially no time-limit on such emotions. It may be, for example, that someone driving home at night suddenly has to stop the car as they are overcome with a sudden burst of sadness. It may be a smell or a comment or a memory flashback, occurring years later, that retriggers a raw burst of emotion. Many assume, incorrectly, that there must be something wrong with them if this occurs long after the death of a loved one. But, of course, nothing could be further from the truth. I remind my patients: 'grief does not do rules'.

The Physical Effects

The body and brain take the hit physically as well as emotionally when you lose someone dear to you. Copious amounts of your stress hormones adrenaline, noradrenaline and especially your chronic stress hormone, glucocortisol, are released, creating many of the physical symptoms which you may experience. Grief also triggers the visual, sensory and auditory parts of the brain. It is helpful to remember that your brain never sleeps, so you may experience some symptoms even when asleep, in the form of dreams or nightmares.

Here are some common physical symptoms you may experience.

1. Symptoms of your acute stress system being activated – giving rise to episodes of palpations, shaking, sweating, stomach in knots and muscle tension.
2. Symptoms of your chronic stress system being triggered – giving rise to fatigue, poor concentration and memory, irritable bowel, tension headaches.
3. Sleep difficulties – these can run the full gamut of insomnia, broken sleep, nightmares and waking up and experiencing some of the hallucinations discussed below.
4. Hallucinations – these are especially common in older age groups, where you may have lost someone with whom you have spent large chunks of your life. They are most likely created by visual, emotional and auditory memories stored in your brain being triggered into action following the death.

One of the commonest physical symptoms is that you

'sense' the person is close to you. There are multiple stories of those who have experienced actual visual images of the deceased person standing before them or hearing their voices or smelling their smell. Many bereaved people find these sensory and other experiences of assistance, but some are frightened by them and worry that they are 'going mad'.

For others who have a strong belief in the afterlife, such images and perceptions only confirm that their loved ones are in a better place and waiting for them. Whilst this is of great comfort to those with such beliefs, the risk is that the person in such situations may decide to actively 'join' them. In general, as time passes, most people will notice that these hallucinations begin to subside.

The Potentially Negative Consequences of Grief

Physical Consequences

Grief can lead to potentially serious physical outcomes. There has been significant research exploring the potential risks of bereavement. One 2011 meta-analysis (which is an overall analysis of the research data on a subject), for example, estimated a 41 per cent increase in mortality in the first six months after the death of a spouse. Clearly bereavement is associated with increased risks to our physical health, especially in the first six to twelve months following the death of a loved one. Any dampening down of the immune system increases our risks of infection and possibly our cancer risks (although evidence for this latter risk is at present weak). It does seem, however, as if the primary hormonal and immune risks relate to the effects of grief on our cardiovascular system. Let's explore this further.

Cardiovascular Risks

It has been known for some time that the death of a loved one can trigger significantly increased risks of cardiovascular conditions in the bereaved.

This is because of the hormonal changes documented earlier, such as rises in our stress hormone glucocortisol, combined with blunting of our normal immune responses. Such effects are most often seen in the first six months to a year following the death. The risk is greatest in the first month of bereavement. They may present as angina, heart attacks (myocardial infarction) or strokes.

How often, following the death of a surviving long-term partner, for example, have you heard the sentence 'he or she died of a broken heart'? What happens in practice here is that their body responds to the raw emotional pain such a loss engenders by triggering inflammatory and other changes in their blood vessels (including high blood pressure and increased blood thickening), giving rise to these vascular incidents, some of which may result in the death of the bereaved partner.

This information does not of course mean that this is an inevitable occurrence. Rather, it emphasizes the importance of looking after your physical health, especially in older age groups, following bereavement, especially if there is any family or prior history of cardiovascular illness.

Psychological Consequences

Grief has an equal capacity to intrude upon your mental health. This is quite understandable as loss, combined with both the massive changes which it can introduce into your life, and the above physical hormonal and immune changes, can place a significant strain on your emotional brain and mind. Whilst, as already discussed, most of us are innately more resilient than we might think, for some the loss does overpower their emotional reserves, and can trigger mental-health difficulties. Let's briefly explore the commonest.

Major Depression

We dealt with this condition earlier in the book. Grief, especially if the effects are prolonged, complex or especially severe, or if the person was especially close to us or if we have a predisposing risk to developing the condition, can trigger a full-blown bout of significant clinical depression.

It is important, however, to distinguish a bout of clinical depression from the almost universal feelings of intense sadness, low mood and other symptoms already discussed, which can be triggered by grief. This distinction is critical to make. The last thing we need to do is to 'medicalize' the grief process, which in essence is a natural, normal human reaction to the loss of someone we love.

If, however, you genuinely feel that you may have slipped into a bout of major depression, seek out the assistance of your family doctor for diagnosis and further assistance.

Anxiety

The loss of someone you love is going to involve, by necessity, the introduction of major changes into your life. Change makes us anxious; as humans, we fear uncertainty above all else. One of the commonest fears, for example, is that of loneliness. Whilst most of us will gradually adapt and make the necessary, if difficult, life changes forced upon us by grief, some of us may become 'stuck'. You may become increasingly fearful, or worry and catastrophise to a level where you struggle to cope. If you have predisposing difficulties with general anxiety or phobias, grief may feed into these. We have already dealt with these in earlier chapters (see page 41). As always, I counsel against the use of medication in such situations and strongly promote CBT techniques, as already laid out, as the best way to manage these conditions.

Self-Harm and Suicide

It has long been recognised that the loss of a loved one can be associated with increased risks of self-harm and especially suicide. One large recent Danish study (2017), reviewing a cohort of over 1.4 million bereaved people over the age of eighteen, found that risks of self-harm, suicide and psychiatric illness were significantly increased over the ten years following the loss, especially in the first year. The risks were highest following the death of a child, the death of a spouse, in younger people, or following a death from suicide, homicide or an accident.

It would be common when grieving over the loss of a loved one to feel on occasions so sad and down that you entertain thoughts of self-harm in the form of 'wanting to be with them' or 'I don't think I can survive on my own without them'. These thoughts are usually short-lived but very distressing.

If you are struggling with a secondary issue, such as a bout of major depression triggered by loss, or are overcome with loneliness if a long-term partner dies, or have lost a child tragically to suicide especially, or any other form of trauma, then such thoughts may harden into more concrete plans as to what you might do to escape your pain. I see such situations as being of equal seriousness to developing significant chest pain, signalling a potential heart attack. For both involve a high risk to you, the person. Both can lead to tragic consequences for both you and those loved ones whom you might leave behind.

If you find yourself heading off down these dark roads, please seek out help urgently, through family, close friends, GP, therapist, bereavement counsellors, or ring one of the many helplines available (see the Resources Section at the back of the book).

You can often prevent yourself reaching such depths of despair by sharing your pain with others. True emotional healing, as we will explore later, will always involve having to be honest with yourself, your pain and loss, and acquiring new ways of coping with the traumatic changes that grief brings. Sometimes, and this is one of those times, you may need to seek out professional or other assistance, to help you with this process. You owe it to both yourself and to those who will have to cope with the consequences of your actions to do so.

The Experience of Grief

With the benefit of over forty years of sharing grief experiences with countless patients of all ages, who have lost loved ones from every known cause, it might be helpful to share with you some insights that I have gained.

1. Unless the death has been long expected (terminal diagnosis or longstanding illness), for most people the immediate impact is that of numbness and disbelief. There may be tears, but many people comment on how they went through the whole wake and burial process in a fog.

2. In Ireland, we traditionally set aside a few days to 'wake' the person, ideally at home or if not at the funeral home. Here the body (often embalmed and in an open coffin) is brought home and the house is open to friends, family members, work colleagues, etc. to pay their respects to

both the deceased and their family. It is a time to remember the life of the person who has died and to celebrate their life, whilst mourning their passing. This allows you time and space to begin the process of grieving and to carry away with you positive memories of this process of saying goodbye. In some countries this may not be possible, but there may be other ways of joining with others to celebrate the life of the person who has left us.

3.   It is important for all, especially children, to see the body, as it allows us to conceptualise better the reality that the person is truly gone.

4.   One of the hardest parts of the initial bereavement process is the period when the burial is over, the crowds are gone and you are left on your own, with the reality that the person you love is gone. You may need to be alone with your own thoughts and personal grief. Or you may prefer to have close family members or friends around, to spend time with them. Whatever you find works best for you is what you should do.

5.   You cannot dodge the reality of the grief process. It is going to be raw, painful and emotionally and physically challenging, no matter how much you would wish it to be otherwise.

6.   I often quote my friend and wonderful raconteur Christy Keneally on the importance of being allowed time and space to rummage around in the rubble of our grief. Sometimes you need time and space to do just this, before trying to pick up the pieces of the rest of your life. Take as much time as you require, if you feel you need to do just this. I worry greatly that we abnormalise those who seem to spend too much time in the rubble

and suggest too easily that they are not 'moving on' fast enough.

7. You may struggle emotionally when meeting people whom you know well, subsequent to the death of your loved one. People frequently do not know what to say and may inadvertently say the wrong thing. Comments such as 'they are in a better place now' or 'you seem to coping so well' can really distress and hurt you if you allow them to. You may also become frustrated and irritable with such individuals. It is better, however, to accept such comments as well-meaning and focus on conserving your emotional energy for the task of 'surviving' the whole process.

8. Another contentious issue is the area of crying – of spilling tears as one recalls and remembers the person we love. Crying is one of the ways that the body attempts to relieve the emotional pain, tension and sadness which builds up on such occasions. Eventually the dam of your inner reserves is pierced and tears flow.

    There is an erroneous belief, which in part goes back to the original five-stage theory of grief, that crying is an essential part of the grief process and that if you are not crying, then you must be, in some manner, blocking out your grief. If you do not cry, it may be seen as unhealthy, with well-intentioned people encouraging you to cry over your loss. Some people will even feel guilty that they have not shed many tears over, perhaps, the death of a parent. The reality is that some of us shed tears easily and others less so. It is simply part of the uniqueness of the human being. It does not mean that you are any less devastated by the loss; rather that you simply do not respond as viscerally as others in the same situation.

9. Others may have the opposite experience of feeling ashamed if they break down in front of people and cry when asked about their loved one. If you find this to be the case, then you are falling into the trap of both rating yourself as 'weak' because you are 'not in control' of your emotions and assuming others will judge you in the same way. The secret, as we discussed in the section on shame, is to develop Unconditional Self-Acceptance and also to accept that crying in such situations is a normal, healthy response to an intolerable loss.

10. One of the biggest obstacles that you may face is well-meaning advice as to how best you should 'move on' following the death. This suggests once again that you should be 'getting over' the loss and that your non-involvement in social or community activities is just an illustration of 'weakness' or that you have 'complex' grief.

    My advice is to set out your own timetable as to when you feel ready to engage again in such activities. Listen to your own inner self, not the advice of those who may not have experienced such a loss in their lives, or who may have ill-informed views on the subject. This advice may also be relevant when dealing with family members, who mean the best but fail to understand your need to rummage in the rubble for a while longer.

11. One of the greatest myths surrounding grief is that 'time is the great healer'. Countless people have shared their frustration and anxiety that time is not healing their pain and sadness, often years after the loss.

The harsh reality is that time does not heal the wound of grief. Rather, over time, we learn to cope better with the pain and loss. It is the growth of our personal inner resilience reserves which finally allows us to continue with our lives, albeit in a much-changed form.

Think of the grief process in this manner, and you may find it less of a struggle. We can cope in life with the truth. It is the false beliefs that cause us difficulties.

12. Another mistaken belief is that if someone close to you dies from a normal cause and you are grieving badly, you should automatically attend a bereavement counsellor or group. This implies that we as human beings lack the inner resilience reserves to manage our own grief reactions.

The reality is that grief is a normal, healthy process, even if incredibly painful and distressing. True emotional healing comes from our own discoveries of what does and doesn't work for us in the grieving process and an acceptance that this will happen when it is right for us. In general, you are best placed to know yourself, and no amount of counselling will allow you to dodge the pain and sadness that comes with grief. You just have to discover how best to manage it.

13. Clearly, complex grief situations do arise, which may require some definite professional intervention and that is absolutely fine too. These can relate to the presence of major depression, significant suicide thoughts or planning, the death of a child, or where there has been an extremely traumatic death such as suicide or homicide. These may require outside assistance as there may be either a secondary mental-health issue such as major

depression, a suicide risk or an associated underlying trauma. Some experts use the term 'complicated grief' to cover such situations. If you do find yourself experiencing such a scenario, then I would strongly recommend that you do go and seek out professional assistance. This is because your normal resilience reserves may not be enough to help you survive in such situations.

14. I am regularly asked, 'How long will this pain go on for?' or 'Will it ever go away?' I have always tried to answer as honestly as I can. For most of us who have lost a loved one, the first year will probably be the worst. Each occasion from anniversaries to birthdays to family gatherings at festive times may bring its own new torrent of sadness, pain and loneliness. The following year, you may notice that you are still getting the same emotional surges at such times but coping slightly better. In some cases, however, such as in suicide bereavement, matters may get worse before they get better.

As the years pass, you will usually notice that you are increasingly coping better, and that the depths of pain and sadness begin to decrease and are most often being triggered by the occasions mentioned.

Your personal grief process will be dictated by your individual nature, the cause and age of the loved one lost, your closeness to the deceased and how well you have been able to adjust to your new situation. Try to experience your grief as it happens to you, and not as you think it should happen.

9. Coping With Your Emotions In Grief

There are two separate, if intertwined, components to the grief process which are often overlooked. These are:

1. The Emotional Component. This relates to our emotional responses to loss.
2. The Change Component. This relates to the significant changes which loss can introduce into the lives of those left behind.

It is critical from the beginning to separate these two components. Emotional healing becomes increasingly complex if you merge both together, rather than managing these two painful processes separately. We can all relate to the first component, but many of us fail to appreciate the role of managing change in coping with loss. We will discuss change in the next chapter. Here, we will focus on how best to manage your emotional responses to loss.

Initial thoughts

Every human being is completely unique, as is our response to loss. The circumstances surrounding your personal loss will be as unique to you as the way in which you will emotionally respond to it. There are also many survivors, struggling with their grief encounters, who wonder if they will ever truly heal the emotional wounds which loss has inflicted upon them.

Is it ever really possible to be emotionally healed if faced with a significant loss in our lives? It is my strong belief, backed up by decades of professional and personal experience, that we can be truly emotionally healed. All of us have innate resilience reservoirs of the psyche and spirit that can be tapped into to help us to survive this painful process and develop new ways of coping with the reality of our loss.

This does not mean that you ever really stop grieving for the person, nor that you will reach a stage where tears may not come flooding back if something triggers an emotional memory. Or that you ever 'forget' the memory of your loved one. Or that a day might not go by, even decades later, where something triggers a fond memory or indeed a sad one.

To apply a physical analogy, suppose you have suffered a deep laceration which is incredibly slow to heal. Eventually the body's repair mechanisms begin to fill in the wound, until the rawness begins to settle and healing begins. But even when the wound has finally closed, you may continue to experience darts of pain at the site of the wound. You will also remain vulnerable to the wound re-opening again if you experience a similar trauma to the area.

Grief behaves likewise from a psychological perspective. How long it takes for the rawness and searing pain to diminish will depend on the depth of the loss, or laceration of the psyche, experienced. It can, on some occasions, take a considerable amount of time for the wound to close. But even when it does, you may still experience intermittent darts of emotional pain and sadness or even a re-opening of the wound of grief if a further loss or trauma occurs.

What this means in practice is that, no matter how bad things may be for you at this moment in time, or how bleak the future without your loved one may seem, there will eventually come a day when emotional healing will slowly but surely take place in your life.

You can assist this process by a better understanding of the experience of grief. This will alert you to the potential pitfalls that may get in the way of learning how to cope with the loss. Just as the healing of a laceration is a natural, normal body process, so too is the healing of the wounds to your heart and spirit which follow loss.

I cannot say it often enough, that the grief process is a normal human response to the loss of someone you love. The issues with grief come when you try to either block or interfere with this process, or get frustrated with the process, believing that you are not 'handling it' properly. Learning to cope with grief, and finding true emotional healing, often means getting out of your own way and allowing grief to take its course.

You may be at the beginning of the grieving process and, if so, this section of the book may be of great assistance, by shining a light on the road you are about to travel and the potholes you may encounter on the way. Others may be further along on their grief journey, perhaps six months, a year or even five to ten years. No matter where you are on the journey, however, the pieces of advice which follow may assist you to emotionally self-heal. Because each person's loss story and grief journey are so different and unique, it is impossible to lay out a healing strategy that could cover every situation. But there are emotional commonalities present in almost all grief experiences which you may find of assistance.

Coping with the Emotions of Grief

Sometimes a death occurs suddenly, such as a loved one dying from a heart attack, stroke, a rapidly advancing cancer or from suicide or trauma. In such situations the commonest initial emotional reaction may be numbness or an absence of emotions. This is the body walling off the pain initially to give us a chance to come to terms with the sudden loss. This is often the case during the first week or so following the death. The bereaved often speak about going through the whole funeral process in a daze. But even at this early stage, the sadness and emotional pain will begin to break through, and you may find yourself crying at times uncontrollably. As a doctor I feel it is important to avoid tranquillizers to get through this period, though they are often recommended with the best of intentions. In my experience, they may block you from experiencing the reality of your loss whilst burying your loved one.

Even if the death is an expected death, such as an elderly person or someone who has died from a terminal diagnosis such as cancer or some other chronic illness, there is still a sense of shock and numbness when they actually die. This surprises many who may have assumed that they have already 'dealt with' their grief. Nothing can really prepare us for that moment when the person is no longer with us.

When the numbness wears off in either situation, the commonest emotions triggered thereafter will be intense sadness and a gnawing internal emotional pain, often accompanied with bouts of crying, a loss of interest in food, difficulties in sleeping, fatigue and lethargy, and just wanting to isolate yourself from the world and all that is in it. On some occasions, there may be anger or guilt or depression or hurt or frustration, depending on the circumstances surrounding the death. Whilst some of these emotions are quite understandable, it is important to try to concentrate more on healthier emotions such as sadness, as this is the cardinal emotion of grief. Sadness, as we discussed in the first chapter, is a healthy negative emotion. It is healthy as it allows the body, brain and mind to cope with your loss. If we block it, then coping becomes more difficult and prolonged. The closer the relationship, the greater the sadness. It is as if we are giving ourselves permission to mourn their loss and come to terms with the reality that they will no longer be present in our lives from then on.

There is little point in trying to put together a timeline for such emotions as there is such a variety of circumstances and situations underlying each loss. It would be completely normal for bouts of intense sadness, low-grade depression-type emotions and symptoms allied to more negative emotions such as those outlined to be present over the first year or two following the death, especially the first six months or so. It has been my experience, however, that in cases such as the death of a child, a much-loved parent, a suicide or major traumatic death, or in the case of the death of a long-term partner, such emotions may be present, even if in diminished strength, many years – even decades – later, following the death.

Let's explore the commoner emotions that you might experience in greater detail and how best to manage them.

Sadness

Let's begin with the healthy negative emotion of sadness. How many of you reading this section have found their heart torn into pieces, their emotional world exploded? No matter what words of comfort are offered by a friend or professional or therapist, there are no shortcuts to coping with the emotional experience of 'grief sadness'. There can be little doubt that the sadness and emotional pain which you may experience will have the capacity on occasions to bring you to your knees. My message of hope, however, is that over time, and with the assistance of this book, you will develop coping mechanisms which will allow you to pick up the pieces of your life and move on. Even if this new life you encounter is different from what went before. It will not be easy, but you can do it. You can emotionally self-heal.

Here are some professional and personal perspectives which might make it easier for you to achieve this goal.

1. Sadness is the body's way of emotionally dealing with your loss, so it is a normal human emotion. It does not matter how intense the emotion is or how long it goes on for, it is critical to accept that it is normal for you to experience it. Please never feel there is something abnormal about you if you feel that you cannot shake off your sadness.

2. Never try to dodge or obstruct this emotion, but accept its embrace, even if intensely painful. For sadness cannot be pushed under the water, it will always come surging back up to meet you, despite your efforts to avoid it. I have known situations, years later, completely out of the blue, where those who have tried to block out this emotion of sadness find themselves suddenly breaking down, totally overcome with sadness and uncontrollable crying as the reality of their loss finally does arrive.

3. Take whatever time you feel necessary to rummage around in the rubble of your grief and loss, no matter how sad you feel. This might mean spending time in places where you feel closest to the person who has died.

Or finding yourself crying seemingly for no reason and accepting that this is OK and normal. Or wishing to spend time on your own, trying to come to terms with your loss. It might mean holding their clothes to your face or looking at that photo which seems to capture their presence best. You do whatever works for you.

4. It is normal to experience the physical symptoms which often go with the emotion of sadness, such as crying or struggling to sleep or eat.

5. Never be afraid to display the emotion of sadness or cry in front of either family members, especially children, or friends or acquaintances in a social situation. Simply explain that you are missing the person. So many in my experience try to hide this emotion, instead of treating it as a normal reaction to loss, which should be understood by us all. Children will find it easier to release their own sadness if you are open about yours.

6. If you find, on the other hand, that you are not a person who easily cries when feeling sad, then this too is both common and fine. You are not 'letting down' the person you love. You are still missing them internally so badly.

7. Even as time moves on and the months and years pass, you will still find your heart buffeted by the winds of grief, with sadness catching you unawares and tears flooding in. This occurred to me personally in a public situation when I, too, had to accept that it was just a sign of the love I had for the person, that the sadness I felt reflected the reality that they were no longer with us, and that my sadness and tears were once again 'normal'. If anything, were they not a reflection of the beauty and humanity within us all?

8.   The good news is that, in general, the bouts of intense sadness do gradually begin to wane over the first few years. Your emotional brain begins to develop increased resilience in coping with memories of your loved one, and is less likely to trigger this emotion. This does not mean that your loss is any the less, nor that you are 'forgetting' the person, but rather that your emotional brain and psyche are adjusting to their loss.

9.   A common question relates to the final resting place of your loved one and how you respond emotionally to spending time there. Some of you may find visiting the grave of a loved one assists you to grieve. You may find yourself feeling sad or crying or simply sensing the presence of your loved one there, which brings you some comfort. For others, however, you may experience a completely different set of emotions when present at the grave. You may feel nothing, or feel angry or frustrated or even depressed that you are struggling to connect with them at their final resting place.

I have often been asked, 'What is wrong with me that I cannot grieve or feel sad at my loved one's last resting place? I know their physical remains are present but do not sense their presence. I often struggle to remain there, feeling increasingly frustrated, even angry. Am I abnormal?'

The answer is that this is completely normal and, more importantly, *you* are normal. Each person is unique and will respond to loss in a manner which makes sense to them. You must discover where you sense the presence of the person most. It may be a room at home, such as the kitchen, study or bedroom which you most associate with them. It may relate to some clothes or other items which were special to them. It may be their texture or smell. It may be a specific place which both of you visited regularly. Wherever you sense the presence of the person you loved, that is where you must go to grieve and leave yourself open to the sadness and, if it helps, allow the tears to flow. Find what works for you, and let it work for you. This might be one of the most important messages in our whole conversation on grief.

10. Finally, one of the most beautiful ways of assisting you in coping with your emotion of sadness is to reflect upon on a quote by C. S. Lewis from *A Grief Observed*, where he wrote about his feelings following the death of his wife Joy: 'The pain I feel now is the happiness I had before. That's the deal.' Would you have given up all the joy, love and wonderful times spent with the person who has died, to stop the pain you are feeling now? For most of us, the answer would be an emphatic 'no'. So, in many ways it is love intermingled with loss that underlies your sadness. Hopefully this beautiful thought might bolster you as you try to cope with the crushing emotional pain you may be feeling at this moment in time.

Guilt

Over the decades, I have found it astonishing how often the emotion of guilt is triggered by the grief process. It is as if our emotional mind and brain simply cannot engage or cope with the enormous waves of sadness and emotional pain. It tries instead to distract us from embracing these healthy negative emotions by diverting our thoughts and efforts into coping with the powerful unhealthy negative emotion of guilt.

This guilt can spill over into so many of the circumstances and issues surrounding either the life or, more commonly, the illness or situation which led to the death of the person we love. We may blame ourselves for not spotting some signs that the person was unwell, or not treating them well in relation to some issue which occurred just before their death. Or that we did not intervene early enough with medical professionals or hospital. Or that we did not spend enough time with the person before they died. There is an almost unending list of potential culprits causing us to self-flagellate, following the death of a loved one.

Guilt is an unhealthy negative emotion, which we discussed in detail earlier. If it is causing you some emotional distress, following the death of a loved one, I recommend re-reading that chapter to understand how to process it (see page 113).

Anger

Along with guilt, anger is another distracting pitfall when struggling with the grief process. I have encountered in my medical practice many grieving individuals and families who have become consumed with anger. This anger is usually directed outwards towards those whom they feel are 'responsible' in some way for the death of their loved one. The commonest culprits are the medical profession, where it may be perceived that they either misdiagnosed some underlying condition or did not manage the condition properly or did not inform them that their loved one was as ill as they were.

On occasions the anger may be directed at other family members whom it is felt did not care sufficiently about the care or health of the loved one. This is so often the case when elderly parents die. There may be anger on other occasions directed towards police or social workers, or indeed on occasions towards life itself.

Quite often the force of the anger can be quite destructive to the person and those around them. It is so much easier to feel anger and hate than face the daunting task of embracing the sadness and emotional pain emanating from our emotional mind. Anger is the second main trickster of grief. I have seen many destroyed by this emotion, with their anger feeding on itself, blotting out any opportunity of emotional healing taking place. It is an extremely unhealthy negative emotion which can destroy us individually and collectively.

Try to understand that your anger is a side-effect of your grief, and that it is distracting you from the important, if painful, work of grieving.

I recommend visiting the earlier pages on anger (see page 149), which will help you to deal with this emotion, so that you can focus instead on grief.

Depression

For the purposes of our discussion here on grief, we are using the term to describe the emotion which is such a regular visitor to those battling the grief process. In this scenario, you have moved from simply struggling to cope to experiencing the more distressing unhealthy negative emotion of depression. It is common to see sadness and depression intermingling at any stage in the grief process. Sadness is simply your emotional response to the reality of your loss. How you are really missing the person who has died. How you are struggling to see how you can move on in your life without their presence. Depression the emotion has more to do with an unhealthy personal self-rating, driven by how poorly you are coping with this sadness.

If you can relate to this emotion in your own experience of grief, here are a few observations which may assist you to manage it better.

1. Just because you may be undergoing regular short periods of low mood following a bereavement does not mean that you are clinically depressed and require medication. This distinction is critical.

2. It is important to distinguish between the emotion of sadness, which is a healthy negative emotion, and depression, which is an unhealthy one and which may be blocking you from engaging with your grief.

3. At the heart of the emotion of depression lies the irrational belief that you are weak or a failure or abnormal or worthless. This belief is of course completely irrational, as human beings cannot be measured or valued in such a manner.

4. But why would the grief process lull you into such damaging personal negative self-ratings? There can be many reasons why this can happen. The commonest reason is where you believe that grief is a time-limited condition and that there must be something 'abnormal' or 'weak' about you if you have not got over the intense sadness and pain after a designated period of grieving. This can lead you to believe that it is 'you' that is the problem and not the 'grief process'. I have seen this on countless occasions cause untold distress to those struggling to deal with their loss.

5. To counteract such thinking requires you to challenge the information that grief is time-limited to begin with. But, on a deeper level, you must learn how to challenge the concept that human beings can be rated at all and embrace the world of Unconditional Self-Acceptance discussed in earlier chapters.

Anxiety

Anxiety, in my experience, can be a common accompanying emotion in grief. The reasons underlying this will be dealt with in the next section, which deals with the massive changes which the loss of a loved one can introduce into your everyday life. All of us worry about change. For change means having to re-adapt our lives, in some form or another, to a completely new situation. This takes us out of our normal comfort zones and casts us, on occasion, completely adrift on the seas of life. Whereas a certain amount of concern or anxiety would be expected following a significant loss, for some survivors their distress levels may rise significantly, as the unhealthy negative emotion of anxiety kicks in.

I encourage you to revisit the pages on anxiety (see page 31), which will help you understand this emotion and work through it. Once you understand that this is a distraction from the pain of grieving, you may find it is easier to deal with your anxiety.

10. Accepting That Your Life Will Never Be The Same

By concentrating almost exclusively, and understandably, on the emotional consequences of grief, are we neglecting the other significant consequence, namely change? The loss of someone we love can blow away in an instant the life to which we have become accustomed. You may struggle to deal with the fact that nothing will ever be the same again. You know that life will never be the same again. You as a person will also be profoundly changed by the loss.

The process of grieving someone with whom you closely shared your life involves not only personal loss, but also the loss of a whole way of life and being. The closer your links to the person who has died are, the more profound these changes may be.

Life is littered with periods of change, where we are forced to keep adapting and altering aspects of ourselves to cope with the onset of new circumstances. Grief, however, presents perhaps the greatest challenge to our innate ability to change and adapt. It is the absolute finality of death, the disappearance of both the person and a way of life built up around them over long periods, sometimes over a lifetime, that brings us to our knees.

There is also an emotional cost to this struggle to cope and adapt to this change. You may become anxious or, on occasion, depressed about the process. You may feel a profound sadness at the loss of not only the person you loved, but the loss of a whole way of life. This element of grief is frequently overlooked as a reason why it can take so long to adjust to life after the death of a loved one. We are mourning the loss of both the person and the life we shared with them. You may become hurt or bitter or angry with life, feeling that a whole world has been suddenly shut down.

The key message from this chapter is processing the understanding that, when you lose someone you loved dearly, you will never be the same again. A special part of you dies with them and can never be replaced. Life will never be the same again. The message of hope from this chapter, however, is that you will build a new life for yourself, following your loss. This new life will be different from that which went before, but you will learn over time to adapt and adjust to this altered reality.

For grief is inherently as much about change as loss. Your ability to survive the process will depend as much on your capacity to adapt to new circumstances as it will on managing your emotional reactions to the loss. This side of the grief process can be difficult to both recognise and manage. For change following loss will involve learning how to cope with a completely new situation and one which you may find extremely distressing. Learning to accept and adapt to your new situation will make the grief process easier to survive.

Here are a few of the commonest changes you may encounter.

The Silence

This is one of the most distressing but least discussed elements of loss. Countless people over decades have confided to me that the biggest change they experienced when someone they loved died was the 'silence'. Never again will they hear the person they loved speak to them. Even more poignantly, never again will they be able to share with them all the news or gossip of the day. Or ask their advice or assistance on matters of import.

This silence is most obviously felt by those who have been in long-term relationships such as marriage or partnerships. The silence is profound if there have been children who have subsequently moved on with their lives. Whilst some can cope with (and by nature are comfortable with) silence, many really struggle in this new scenario.

I have heard patients describe the period of silence that follows when the funeral services are over and family and well-wishers are gone as one of the most distressing periods they encounter in the early stages of grief. The silence can be deafening. What upsets most is the dawning realisation that never again will the silence be broken by the voice of the person they loved.

There is a special quality to the relationship between long-term partners that makes this silence even more poignant and distressing. As time passes and the period of grief extends, the loss of this communication that was so normal and natural can engender even greater sadness and pain. We mourn not only the loss of the person, but the loss of the sound of their voice and the joy of sharing with them every aspect of our lives.

But it is not only the remaining partner in a long-term relationship who may struggle in this manner. The silence created by the inability of a parent to speak to a child or young adult who is no longer with us, can also be overwhelming. The loss of the constant daily or weekly telephone calls to your recently deceased mother or father. The loss of regular communications with a sibling who is gone. The silence when a close friend, with whom you have shared much of your life, dies.

It would be common, in my experience, especially where the relationship with the person was close, that the grieving person spends much of their time filling in the silence by talking to the person when alone, as if they were there beside them. Some of you may feel embarrassed to share this information. Does this mean that you are going crazy? The answer is emphatically 'no'. This is a normal and healthy way of dealing with your loss.

If talking out loud to your lost loved one helps you to cope better with the loss of such an important avenue of communication, then carry on and never let anyone convince you otherwise. Others have shared their distress, after a period of time, that they could no longer remember the voice of their loved ones. It is often useful in such situations to listen to any recordings or videos of the person from the past to reignite the connection.

Are there any ways to cope better with the deafening silence which can follow the loss of someone we cared deeply for? Here are some suggestions.

1. Accept the silence from the beginning as a reality. You will no longer be able to share with the person you loved many of the topics already mentioned above. This is hard to accept but becomes easier if you can learn to do so and use other techniques to cope with their loss.
2. Do not be afraid to talk to the person that is gone, in any way you feel. Shout at them, cry with them, talk aloud as much as you wish, share with them things that you are struggling with and so on. This has the dual effect of helping you get things off your chest and helping you to feel their presence around you.

3. Some people have found that they prefer to keep a radio or a TV or even music constantly playing in the background, to drown out the silence. Others are comfortable with leaving the silence. You must choose which one works for you.

4. If you do have family or close friends or good neighbours, do not be afraid to let them know that you are struggling with silence, if it is an issue. Try to either get them to visit you or even better visit them.

5. As time passes and you find yourself coping better with the emotions of grief, you might find it useful to spend increasing amounts of time out of the house, socialising with others. For some, the house can otherwise become a cage of silence. Once again, do this at your own speed and in whatever form you choose.

Your Social World

The loss of a loved one can lead to the disintegration of the social world that you may have built up around them. This can be especially difficult for those who lose a long-term partner with whom they may have shared common interests and social contacts. It can be especially distressing for some men who lose their female partners, as women are usually better at building and maintaining a social structure. But women, too, can really feel the loss of their male partner when interacting socially, and equally struggle with this change.

This alteration in your social circumstances can present itself in many different settings. If your socialising was done as a couple, you may struggle to engage in such situations in their absence. You may find that it was your departed partner who was the link in a particular social relationship and that when they died, the link died with them. You may feel embarrassed or ashamed to be the 'odd one out' when asked to join a social occasion such as a party or wedding. You may find yourself becoming so distressed emotionally when asked about your deceased partner that you avoid such social events. You may find that being present at such occasions triggers an intense inner loneliness, as you pine for their automatic support and back-up. Such social events often remind you just how much everything in your life has changed.

One area of your social world which is especially disrupted, and one which is rarely discussed, is how the loss of a loved one, especially a long-term partner or parent, affects holidays. The sudden change in your social circumstances in such situations can be profound. For some, holidays or vacations become something to be dreaded rather than enjoyed. Nowhere is the absence of the person you love going to be felt more keenly than when removed from normal routines during such occasions. The silence, the absence of someone to share the experiences with, the meal on your own, the absence of laughter and joy, all conspire to worsen how you may feel emotionally at such times.

It is not only partners who may struggle with the change in social circumstances. There can be equal difficulties with close siblings or friends who have spent significant amounts of time together in social situations. Or where parents have spent time socialising with their adult children or vice versa.

Those who have lost someone to suicide can find this change in their social circumstances extremely challenging, as do those who have lost someone to a sudden trauma. Parents who have lost a child may especially struggle to cope socially with their new circumstances.

There is little that can be done to soften or override this massive change in your social circumstances, but here are a few suggestions.

1. Accept that one of the biggest challenges that you will face following loss is having to adapt to what will inevitably be a new situation socially. If shut off from specific social situations as the link was with your loved one or partner, then accept that this is part of the change. This reduces your emotions of anxiety and frustration. You may in time, when you feel ready to do so, reach out socially to different groups and individuals and form new relationships. Safeguard the close social relationships you do have.

2. Accept that there will be times when on your own at social occasions, perhaps with other couples, that you may find yourself feeling lonely or dislocated, especially at the beginning of your grief journey. This is normal and should be accepted as such. As time progresses, however, you will rebuild your social life and hopefully your feelings of loneliness may dissipate.

3. If planning to go on a holiday break, it is critical to accept that such vacations will now be different, for like everything else in your life, all is changed utterly. It might be sensible to go with close family members or friends to reduce the loneliness and isolation that you may experience. If the latter is not possible, then another option is to go on interesting group holiday packages, where you may meet others in a similar situation.

4. Once again, I reiterate my warning about the house sometimes being an unhealthy space to spend too much time alone in. When you feel ready to do so, it is healthier to seek out social contact with friends, neighbours, family members or others, all of whom will provide you with the emotional nourishment which as human beings we need.

From the beginning of your grieving period, try to ensure that socially you look outwards and not inwards.

Domestic Changes

Another area of life which often changes dramatically relates to your domestic situation. You may find yourself suddenly living on your own in a house or apartment which was previously looked after by you and your loved one. It can relate to major changes in your financial situation, as when one partner dies, some financial support to the household may die with them. This can cause great anxiety and distress. In other situations, tasks in the house may have been split, with one party more comfortable perhaps in dealing with finances or practical issues and the other with domestic issues. Now the remaining partner finds themselves having to take on all such chores or tasks themselves. There can be difficult decisions as to whether to stay on alone in the house or move into a smaller or different social dwelling.

You may find yourself having to deal with domestic issues relating to a partner or parent who has died, ranging from dealing with their estate to deciding what to do with their belongings.

An especially challenging domestic scenario can develop if a parent of young or adolescent children is suddenly left to take on the responsibility of rearing them on their own. This can be a daunting change which can lead to significant anxiety and frustration as the remaining parent tries to adapt to this new scenario without the support and love of the person whom they have lost.

Another distressing domestic issue which can arise, especially in the first year following the death of a loved one, is what to do with their personal belongings. In many cases, there can be huge sentimental value attached to clothes, or favourite chairs or music collections or sporting items. One of the commonest causes of distress to the bereaved person is where someone, either a family member or friend, is encouraging them to throw out items of sentimental value or to send them to charity. The idea is that if they do so quickly, it will assist them to deal better with their grief and make a faster recovery back to normal. Nothing could be further away from the truth. The reality is that keeping such items of personal value can be for some a critical component for long-term emotional healing.

Another domestic issue and one that can lead to great distress is where there is a dispute amongst so-called loved ones about the estate or will of the person who has died. Over forty years of being a family doctor, I have been shocked at how quickly these financial disagreements can escalate, and how devastating they can be. It can be yet another source of change and confusion when those you believed would support and understand you in your time of grief seem to turn against you.

There are many other areas of your life that you will have to adapt to and alter when grief comes calling, but the above constitute, in my experience, the major changes that you will encounter.

Here are a few practical coping suggestions, which you may find useful.

1. The best piece of advice that I can give to anyone struggling with some or all these domestic changes following the loss of a loved one is to make no major decisions for a minimum of one year unless it is essential to do so. In other words, do not sell the house, move to a new neighbourhood or make any other major domestic decisions while you are still in the immediate period of bereavement. This will give you some breathing space and time to try to decide what changes work for you, while maintaining

some of the routine and familiarity around you. I would apply this advice right across the whole spectrum of your domestic world.

2. From the beginning, find refuge in all the domestic, daily household and other chores. Use them as a sort of mindfulness exercise, allowing your emotional mind some time off from the turbulent emotions swilling around in your brain. Routine can be a great comfort to you when it feels as if everything else in your life has become untethered.

3. If you are not normally an independent soul, then try to learn to look after yourself, including staying in the house on your own if a long-term partner has died. This will make you more resilient to cope with the many changes and adaptions that your loss will force upon you. But each person must work out what is best for them, so if you struggle with the above, then perhaps explore other options.

4. A common dilemma, as already noted, is what to do with the possessions of the person you love. I advise that it is you, the person left behind, who must decide how best to deal with such possessions and not any well-meaning family members or close friends. If you wish to hold on to these possessions for a certain period or indefinitely, both options are fine. We know from an emotional memory point of view that senses such as touch and smell are powerful reminders of the person who has left us. Smell is the most basic and powerful sense in the body and a strong trigger for your emotional memory. You may wish to hold on to clothes or furniture or other objects which retain those memories. It is not a sign that you are abnormal or not grieving properly if you do hold on to them. Go with

your heart. You will know yourself when it might be time to gradually let some of them go.

5. If struggling with financial, legal or other significant changes domestically, seek out advice from someone you trust who is a professional in the area and work with them to resolve any difficulties.

11. Coping With The Death Of A Partner

One of the greatest gifts or blessings that life can bestow upon us is the gift of a fulfilling relationship. It is not a gift that should ever be taken lightly or for granted. To have someone beside you whilst dealing with the myriad problems and difficulties that life can throw at us. Who will share the highs and lows, the joys and the disappointments. Who will love you unconditionally, come what may. If you are lucky enough to find such a partner, then you are indeed much blessed.

But what happens when you lose this treasured and much-loved partner? In this chapter we are going to explore the specific issues that this may cause, and later will meet Peter, who has lost his life-time partner Jane, and see how he learns to come to terms with both his loss and the changes which it introduces into his life.

There are two major scenarios that life can throw at you. The first is losing your partner at a relatively young age, the second is losing a long-term partner later in life. Both are equally devastating, but the issues that you may have to face following each loss can be different.

Coping with the Loss of a Partner at an Early Stage of Life

There is something unnatural about someone you know and love dying prematurely, perhaps in their thirties or forties or on occasion even younger. It is not the natural order of life when someone young and vibrant is taken from us through illness or trauma. Unexpected illness such as cancer, premature heart attacks, strokes or road-traffic or other accidents would be typical examples of what might cause them to die prematurely. Such conditions often occur suddenly and there may be little time to say goodbye. So, allied to the grief reaction, you must also cope with the trauma of their premature death and the massive changes in your life which will ensue.

A further complicating dimension which can make the loss of a partner at this stage still more distressing is if they have left behind small children or adolescents. The remaining partner, in the middle of their own grief, is left with the difficult task of rearing the surviving children during the grieving process.

Losing a partner at this stage of life is devastating and the grief process will present significant emotional and change challenges. I am sometimes asked if men or women cope better with this distressing scenario. My personal belief is that nobody, male or female, ever copes well with such a loss. It is too raw and traumatic for the human spirit to experience without significant after-effects. Both men and women struggle with the emotional rollercoaster of the grief process which follows, but I have found women are often better at coping with the changes that such a loss will introduce into their lives. In my experience, women are better at adapting to such situations than men.

On the emotional front, following on from the inevitable

numbness which is your body's natural anaesthetic to cope with the initial wave of grief, overwhelming sadness and emotional pain will, as always, be the primary emotions unleashed by the loss. There can also be significant issues with anger, hurt and guilt. We have already discussed in detail in chapter nine how best to cope with these emotions (see pages 191–203), and I urge you to revisit these sections and read them carefully.

It is also important to watch out for some of the negative behavioural patterns which can follow on from these emotions, such as isolating oneself, drinking more, lashing out at others and life and so on. None of these will assist you in coping with or managing your loss.

It can be extremely difficult to cope with the flood of emotions that losing a partner at this stage of life releases. This sometimes pales into insignificance, however, when faced with the raft of changes that are catapulted into your life at such times. These changes affect every part of our being. You will have to deal with the loss of support, emotionally, financially, socially and otherwise that would normally be available from your partner. Sometimes the task may seem so overwhelming that you may feel like just downing tools and giving up. But in life we have no option but to cope, especially if we are now the sole carer for children. We must keep going, if not for ourselves, then for the sake of those we love and who depend on us. At times it may seem impossible, but you can do it. The human spirit is indomitable.

Here are some insights to make coping with such changes a little easier.

1. Imagine the change element of the grief process as a journey and, from the beginning, just think of moving forward one step at a time. Don't project too far into the future

and begin catastrophising. Just think about the immediate next step, and take it. Start with the simple tasks and gradually move on to the more complex and distressing ones.

2. Accept from the beginning that nothing will ever be the same; neither you as a person nor the situation that you now find yourself in. This acceptance is key to adapting to and surviving this loss.

3. Keep focusing on the daily routine of getting up, preparing meals, looking after the children or adolescents if present, doing routine domestic chores, returning to the workplace even if numb and feeling incapable of carrying on. Slowly but surely, routine will save us from going over the edge and create some form of stable platform that will allow us to pick up the broken pieces of our lives.

4. Try to draw on any offers of assistance from any source, whether family, loved ones, close friends, professionals or the workplace. They cannot share your grief but may make coping with the changes you will have to make more tolerable.

5. One of the biggest changes may be the arrival of loneliness. Without the support of a partner, you may feel trapped by the stage of life that you find yourself in, especially if you have children that you are now totally responsible for. Some of the most poignant communication I've received as a mental-health commentator on the radio relates to the loneliness that men especially feel when partners die in such circumstances. But such loneliness is not just confined to men, as women too can be crushed by it. See page 210 for a reminder on how to deal with this loneliness.

6. It is helpful to reflect on the experiences of others who have survived the loss of a partner at this stage of life.

Most say that while adapting to the emotional side of the grieving process took time, they found they adapted to the changed domestic circumstances much more quickly through necessity. This is not to say that they found it easy, as it can be very distressing, but the demands of a family and a working life can keep us going from day to day.

7. I have always questioned the term 'time is a great healer' as I believe that in relation to our emotional responses to grief, this statement is false. If you lose a partner at this phase of your life, it is highly unlikely that time will ever heal the sadness and pain. However, a longstanding maxim of mine is that 'time is the great facilitator of adaptation'. The human body, brain, mind and spirit seem to be built on a platform that facilitates adaptation. This allows you to change and adjust to new circumstances and build such changes into your everyday life, often more rapidly than you might have thought possible. You will learn to adjust, adapt and eventually see the pieces of your 'new life' taking place, in whatever form that may take. But it will be different from that which went before.

8. When coping and adapting seem impossible, remember that it is possible to put up with almost anything in life if it is in your own interests or in the interests of those you love.

Coping with the Loss of a Long-Term Partner at a Later Stage of Life

One of the greatest joys that life can bestow on those lucky enough to experience it is that of living and sharing one's life with another human being in a loving long-term partnership. A constant presence in your life from the beginning, someone who has shared a substantial portion of their life with you. Who has experienced the best and worst of both you and life itself, the highs, the lows and all in-between. With whom you may have reared children and seen them progress in their own lives to become independent self-sufficient adults, with perhaps their own relationships. With whom you have experienced and survived all that life can throw at us, in the form of illness, grief, disappointments, combined with those special, never to be forgotten, joyous moments. Someone who has loved you dearly and completely and vice versa. Who has accepted you unconditionally, for the flawed, unique, special human being that you are.

It follows that one of the greatest blows for those who have experienced this unique relationship is to lose this special person and all that goes with that loss. I am referring in this section primarily to those who are in their late fifties onwards. 'Devastating' and 'life-changing' are just some of the terms to describe the inner devastation and emotional barrenness that such a loss induces within us. There are simply no words to describe how this loss can alter and change us as human beings or emotionally describe how we feel, in the months and years following on from losing a long-term partner. It is as if a large piece of your heart is torn out of your chest and dies alongside the person who has left you.

Emotionally, there are many similarities between losing a partner earlier in life and later, but there are also some differences. As before, you may find yourself initially numb, but once this wears off, the waves of sadness will sweep over you, and you may feel like screaming to relieve the emotional pain which will often accompany it. Some have confided how the urge to relieve this pain and to 'be with' the person who has died can sometimes be overwhelming.

It is vital to recognise that this sadness and pain is simply your body, brain and emotional mind attempting to cope with the loss of your loved one. It is facile to say that you will eventually 'get over' the pain. The reality is that over a long period of time, your emotional mind will gradually adjust to carrying this load of grief and sadness and it becomes a little easier to cope with. Anyone who tells you otherwise has probably never experienced such a grievous loss. Remember that going down other dark roads such as suicide will simply pass on this load to those who love us, and that irrespective of how you may feel at a moment in time, you will learn to 'survive'. For survival must be your first objective, when faced with such an overwhelming loss. After that, you are looking at trying to rebuild a new life which will be, by necessity, fundamentally different from the one which went before.

Apart from the primary emotion of sadness, you may also experience unhealthy negative emotions such as depression, anxiety as to the future without your loved one, anger at others or life, frustration and on occasions even shame as you struggle with the social changes which will inevitably ensue following your loss. We have already explored how to manage these emotions on pages 191–203 and I suggest you revisit those sections.

As with losing a partner earlier in life, the second major challenge is how to cope and manage with the enormous life changes which inevitably follow. These may involve loneliness combined with significant domestic and social changes, all of which will need you to adapt. You will probably find loneliness to be the greatest challenge. How often in a long-term relationship are both parties so entwined from an empathy perspective that they seem to know what the other is thinking, and may even finish a sentence which the other has begun? When you are used to sharing every small item of news, gossip or otherwise with the other, the silence can be deafening. I addressed how best to cope with the silence of an empty home on page 205, and you will find useful advice there.

Sometimes these inevitable domestic and social changes have a more devastating effect upon us than the emotional tsunami of grief itself. An extra complicating factor, in a modern context, is how children and wider family in such situations may be widely dispersed, so we miss their nourishment and support in such situations. You may have to rely more on your own reserves to survive both the emotional impact and significant changes which may follow on from your loss. Many of the suggestions detailed earlier as to how best to cope with both the emotional and change side of grieving over the death of a partner apply also to this situation as well: see page 191.

There may be some long-term relationships which were dysfunctional, or where partners for various reasons had drifted apart, where the death may not leave such an emotional impact on the bereaved partner. Even in these situations. however, there will be some emotional and change effects. There may be less sadness, but perhaps more regret or even guilt. The same range of domestic and social change may still apply. The likelihood, however, is that in such relationships the grief process may not be as severe or as long-lasting.

Let's now meet Peter, who has suffered a later-life partner loss, and discover how he achieves a form of emotional healing which allows him to pick up the pieces of his life and move on.

Peter's Story

Peter, a sixty-six-year-old civil servant, had just reached retirement age when his wife, Jane, died. He and Jane had been married for over forty years and were inseparable. They had reared three children, presently scattered between Australia, the USA and UK, all happily ensconced in stable relationships. Peter and Jane, a retired teacher, had experienced all the highs and lows that life could throw at them, including the latter surviving a cancer scare ten years previously, following which she was given the all-clear. They had been planning for years for the retirement phase of their lives, even purchasing a large camper van for proposed long trips around Europe.

They had always had a healthy relationship, spending time together, whilst keeping up individually with friends and acquaintances and taking part in separate activities. Every piece of news and gossip was shared over the dinner table, with both taking an active interest in politics and current affairs. As Jane revealed to some close friends, they 'almost knew what the other was thinking'.

Whilst busily planning their future life, tragedy struck. A month after Peter's retirement, Jane began to feel unwell and within weeks was diagnosed with advanced metastatic cancer, unresponsive to treatment. The original cancer had silently returned and, with it, their hopes and dreams for the future evaporated. Within two months, Jane was dead. For Peter, these months passed in a blur of doctors and palliative-care nurses. His memories are of trying to keep Jane's spirits up while coping with the grief reactions of their three children and then the awful few days of trying to keep it together during the wake, funeral and burial service. Everybody was so kind, but he found himself numb and struggling to keep it together until all was over.

What kept him going throughout the whole process was the love and understanding that poured out of Jane, despite her terminal state. They spent every waking moment together, clinging to each other, trying to make sense of the nightmare they found themselves inhabiting. Jane, a strong Catholic who was not afraid of dying and knew that she was going somewhere special, reassured him that they would both be together eventually. Peter, who had always struggled with the concept of God or an afterlife, was happy to go along with her beliefs, as it was helping Jane cope with her impending death. But deep inside, he was torn apart by waves of numbness, confusion and despair.

After the funeral, the children returned to their own lives, and close friends and wider family members drifted back to theirs. Peter found himself at home, on his own, experiencing, for the first time in over forty years, the sound of absolute silence. And with it came the tears. For Peter belonged to the 'old school', where real men never reveal their emotions in public and especially never cry. All Peter wanted at that moment was to be with Jane.

The year which followed was one of the most difficult of his life. Emotionally, he alternated between bouts of unbearable emotional pain and sadness, which he found occurred in social situations as well as at home alone. He was ashamed and embarrassed by this. Initially he was angry at both life and the medical profession for not being able to predict that the cancer would return. Thankfully a chat with his family doctor quickly cleared that hurdle. He became increasingly anxious, however, as to how he was going to cope with a future which he saw as increasingly bleak and hopeless.

Things, however, got worse for Peter after the first year, when both his own children and indeed others began to imply that he should be 'over things' and that it was time for him to 'move on'. They even suggested that maybe he needed to try to meet somebody else to share the remainder of his life with. This made him both feel guilty and depressed. He began to withdraw socially, spending more time on his own, at home. He found himself drinking more to blot out the pain. Despite well-meaning friends reassuring him that time would heal the sadness and pain, Peter found both emotions intensifying rather than easing. He could see no way out of the nightmare he found himself in.

And that was just the emotional side of losing Jane. Nothing could have prepared him for the domestic and social changes that her loss introduced into his life. Years before, a good friend, John, had intimated to him that the hardest thing for him, following the death of his partner, was the upheaval to his domestic and social life. Peter often reflected on those words in the years which followed Jane's death.

The biggest change related to the silence and the loneliness, which were almost unbearable. He constantly sensed he could hear her voice in his ear and, despite himself, found he was having conversations with her out loud, especially at the kitchen table. In the beginning, he had some visual hallucinations, especially at night and in the early morning, and thought that he was going mad. Thankfully his family doctor reassured him that these were normal following the death of a loved one. Over time, these faded but the silence and loneliness remained. Peter discovered that the radio became his closest friend as it stopped him from going completely over the edge from the sound of silence.

On the domestic and social fronts, the changes were equally challenging. Jane had always managed the practical and financial side of the household, whilst he loved preparing meals, hoovering the house and taking care of the garden. They had always shared the other chores. Now, he was trying to cope with all these activities on his own, whilst feeling emotionally devastated. He found himself constantly breaking down into tears, feeling both frustrated and depressed with himself for not coping better.

Socially, he was really struggling, for Peter had always been a quiet man, very comfortable to allow Jane to do all the chatting in company, happy to be just present with her on such occasions. He now found himself dreading such social occasions without her. This was compounded by his inability to speak about Jane publicly without becoming distressed or crying. He began to avoid such situations, which only worsened his sense of isolation. He had also pulled back from many of his normal hobbies and activities for the same reasons. He saw himself through the eyes of others as odd or weird, as he believed normal people did not respond to loss in such a manner. This made him feel increasingly depressed and ashamed socially.

He no longer looked forward to holidays as Jane would not be there. There was nobody to share those special moments with. The camper van stayed stubbornly immobile in the driveway with Peter considering selling it. What was the point of it all now? His dreams were in ashes.

He became increasingly agnostic and bitter. The belief that Jane was 'out there' somewhere in a 'better place' was, in his mind, a delusion. This added to his pain and sadness, and his sense of life being purposeless and having no meaning with Jane no longer sharing it with him. He also viewed himself as a weak person, someone who was unable to 'get over' his grief, unlike countless others in his situation.

He was seriously considering taking his own life to end the relentless waves of pain and sadness. His mood was dropping, especially following periods of heavy drinking, and this was adding to his emotional pain. Friends noticed that he was withdrawing and tried to persuade him to seek out professional assistance or bereavement counselling, but Peter shrugged off their well-meaning advice.

Luckily, his daughter, sensing from telephone calls that all was not well, arrived home suddenly for a visit, with his five-year-old granddaughter in tow. As Peter was playing with her in the garden, he suddenly caught a glimpse of Jane in her face as she smiled at him and gave him a hug. It was as if a beam of light suddenly shot through the darkness, which had been all-consuming. It was as if Jane herself was sending him a message, that there was a future, and that future was in front of his eyes. He broke down in tears in front of his daughter and shared with her the sadness and pain which had been consuming him. It was a cathartic experience for both of them.

They attended his family doctor together, where Peter revealed how close he had come to 'joining Jane'. She suggested that perhaps Peter might like to chat to a colleague, Dr Jim. She did not feel that Peter was clinically depressed but did recommend ceasing alcohol and beginning a new exercise regimen, which he agreed to do.

Two weeks later, Peter is sitting in front of Dr Jim and pouring out his story, interspersed with tears. His journey towards emotional healing is about to begin. Dr Jim listens empathetically and reassures Peter that what has occurred to him is common and connected to the whole process of grieving. He discusses how emotionally painful this process can be and how difficult to adapt to the changed landscape that loss can create.

'The first lesson of grief,' he explains, 'is that neither you, nor the life you have led, will ever be the same again.'

Peter, sensing an empathy bond, asks if there are some techniques or approaches which might assist him to cope better with his loss. Dr Jim promises to assist him to do just that, using CBT techniques.

He explains about rational and irrational beliefs and lays out the ABC concepts, explaining how they will employ this system to locate and manage his irrational beliefs (see page 24 for an explanation of these). They decide to use Jane's death as the trigger.

'How did this make you feel emotionally?' asks Dr Jim.

Peter initially struggles to identify the relevant emotions, so together they explore the emotional menu to assist him in answering this question. Peter finally details his emotions as follows. 'Initially I just felt numb, but then came the sadness, emotional pain, anxiety, anger for a short period and then finally depression and shame. It has been a real rollercoaster of emotions and not one I want to experience again.'

'What were your behavioural responses to these emotions?' asks Dr Jim. 'What did you do when you felt like this?'

Peter admits to a mixture of unhealthy behaviours, where he found himself spending increasing amounts of time alone, withdrawing from friends and wider family, catastrophising about the awful future he could envisage for himself without Jane, drinking more, stopping looking after his physical health and appearances, eating junk food, avoiding social situations, railing against the world and an imaginary God, and finally seeking out information as to how best to end it all.

'How did these emotions make you feel physically?' asks Dr Jim.

'Just awful,' Peter replies. 'Constantly tired, struggling with sleep, couldn't concentrate on anything, had no motivation, experienced tension headaches and lost my appetite for long periods.'

They decide to add this information to Peter's ABC:

A – Activating Event:
- Trigger: Jane's death from terminal cancer
- Inference/danger:

B – Belief/Demands:

C – Consequences:
- Emotional reactions: sadness; emotional pain; anxiety; depression; shame and hurt

- Physical reactions: fatigue; poor concentration; sleep difficulties; lack of motivation; tension headaches and anorexia
- Behaviour: spending increasing time on his own; withdrawing socially; catastrophising about his future; drinking excessively; railing against 'God' and life; eating junk food; refusing to look after physical health; seeking out self-harm sites.

Dr Jim then explores what inferences that Peter had taken from the death of Jane had led to the mixture of healthy and unhealthy negative emotions already described.

He firstly asks Peter, 'What was it about Jane's death that caused you to feel so much sadness and emotional pain?'

'That she is truly gone, and that I will never see or hear from her again,' he replies. 'I am not a believer, so cannot console myself that I will see her in another life, for I believe that this is all there is.'

With that, Peter breaks down in tears, overwhelmed by the enormity of his loss. Dr Jim empathizes with him and allows him some time to grieve, before probing further.

'Was there anything else about her death that continues to make you sad, other than the major gap her death has left in your life?'

Peter understands what Dr Jim is asking, 'If you are talking about the loss of all those years we could have had together, or the wonderful shared experiences we would have experienced if Jane were still alive, then the answer is unequivocally yes, that makes me so sad.'

This leads to a discussion of how Peter felt cheated of all the potentially happy years that Jane and he could have enjoyed if death had not spoiled the party.

'This loss of our future is almost as great as losing Jane herself,' he admits sadly.

'And what was it about her death that caused you to feel depressed?' asks Dr Jim.

'I have always thought of myself as being a strong person,' Peter replies. 'So I could not accept that I was unable to get over Jane's death as fast as other people I know who have experienced similar losses. To me, this is a sign of weakness.'

'And what was it about her death that made you feel ashamed?' Dr Jim asks.

'It was what other people must think of me, as I keep breaking down crying in front of them,' he replies. 'Real men don't show their feelings in such a manner, so I assume they are seeing me the way I see myself, as weak and useless.'

'And what about her death caused you to feel anxious?' asks Dr Jim.

'It was the uncertainty about the future that lies ahead for me,' Peter replies. 'Before her death, I believed that I was in control of life and knew where Jane and I were going. Since her death, I no longer feel in control of anything and have no idea how it is all going to end. But my biggest worry is that I will live the rest of my life alone, unloved and permanently bitter.'

'And what about it made you feel hurt?' asks Dr Jim.

'It was so unfair,' Peter replies. 'It was as if life was kicking me in the teeth. I know so many couples of my age group who are looking forward to years of happiness together, so why me? What have I done to the universe that I deserve life treating me like this?'

'Let's now examine what irrational beliefs were triggered by Jane's death and the inferences you assigned to it,' says Dr Jim. 'This usually takes the form of some absolute demands you were making about the trigger, which in this case was her death.'

With Dr Jim's assistance, Peter decides that it was completely rational, human and healthy to mourn the loss of Jane, but that they needed to have a discussion as to what the normal course of such a loss would look like. Dr Jim promises to elaborate on this further at a later stage. They then proceed to explore the other irrational beliefs and demands he was making about Jane's death.

They decide that Peter's belief in relation to his emotion of depression was 'that because he had not "got over" his sadness and grief that he was weak and useless. His demand in relation to anxiety was that 'he must not finish up alone, unloved and bitter, as if this happens, he would be a failure.' In relation to shame, his demand was that 'he must accept the harsh judgements of others when they see him crying in public.' Finally, in relation to hurt, his demands were that 'he should be treated fairly,' and that 'life should treat him fairly.'

They add this information to complete Peter's ABC:

A – Activating Event:
- Trigger: Jane's death from terminal cancer
- Inference/danger: that I will never see Jane again as I am a non-believer; that I have been not only been robbed of her but of all of the potential years of happiness we could have enjoyed; that because I have not 'got over' my grief; I am 'weak' and 'useless'; I might end up alone, lonely and bitter; others would judge me as weak and weird when I break down crying in front of them; I am being treated unfairly by life, as others in similar situations did not experience such a loss.

B – Belief/Demands:
- 'Because I have not "got over" my grief and sadness, I am weak and useless.' 'I must not be left on my own, alone

and bitter, if this happens, I am a failure for letting it happen.' 'People will judge me harshly and I must accept their negative judgements. 'I must be treated fairly, and life must treat me fairly.'

C – Consequences:

- Emotional reactions: sadness; emotional pain; anxiety; depression; shame and hurt
- Physical reactions: fatigue; poor concentration; sleep difficulties; lack of motivation; tension headaches and anorexia
- Behaviour: spending increasing time on his own; withdrawing socially; catastrophising about his future; drinking excessively; railing against 'God' and life; eating junk food; refusing to look after physical health; seeking out self-harm sites.

Peter felt, on reading what he had written, that he now had a better understanding of why he was thinking, feeling and behaving the way he was.

'But how can I progress from here?' he asks.

They agree that it is futile to challenge Peter's various emotions. 'That is just the way we feel about something. Trying to feel differently than we do is a pointless exercise,' explains Dr Jim. 'However, we can learn much by exploring and challenging your unhealthy thinking and behavioural patterns.'

They begin by Dr Jim challenging Peter's behaviours, asking, 'Are they in any way assisting you in relation to this situation?'

Peter agrees that his unhealthy lifestyle patterns in relation to alcohol, diet and exercise – and especially his tendency to avoid social situations, which only added to his loneliness and isolation – were unhelpful. They also agreed that self-harm would simply pass on his current sadness and difficulties to those he would leave behind. Peter admits that Jane would have been devastated if she had been aware that her passing could have created such a crisis.

The real work begins, however, when Dr Jim challenges Peter's beliefs and demands. They begin with a major discussion on the whole grief process. Peter is both astounded and relieved to discover that what he is feeling in terms of sadness and loss is both normal and ongoing, for both himself and all those undergoing a similar experience.

'Are you saying that I will always experience such sadness and pain?' he asks.

'You will never really stop grieving or feeling sad or indeed having sudden outbursts of crying if something reminds you of Jane,' answers Dr Jim. 'But as time passes, you will learn how to adapt to carrying this burden of grief.'

He elaborates further. 'Your grief process involves not only the loss of Jane, the person you love, but also of the future life that you would have shared together. It involves therefore not only coping with the sadness, but also with the enormous changes that her loss has introduced into your life. Your life will never be the same. You will never be the same. If you can learn to understand and accept this reality, you will find that you will survive and manage her loss and carve out a different life for yourself. That is the best that any of us can hope for in such a situation.'

This is a life-altering insight for Peter as he realizes how his false perceptions about how he should experience the grief process had been heaping further emotional distress on himself and those he loved. The major insight was that he would never be the same again, as something precious and irreplaceable had indeed been taken from him. He also grasps that he would continue to have periods of sadness and crying, but that was not only 'OK' but 'normal'. He feels as if a great weight has been removed from his shoulders.

This leads to further discussions on his belief (underlying his emotion of depression) that 'because he had not "got over" his sadness he was "weak" and "useless". This leads to an interesting discussion where Dr Jim challenges Peter as to whether human beings can be rated or measured or defined in such terms. He introduces Peter to the concept of Unconditional Self-Acceptance, where he would learn to 'accept himself for the special unique person that he was and only define his behaviour as weak or useless or abnormal' and gives him the Unconditional Self-Acceptance Exercise to practice over the coming months (see page 68).

Peter now sees that his demand (underlying his emotion of shame) that 'he must accept the negative judgements of others, if for example breaking down and crying' was equally unhealthy.

'If I grasp what you are saying about rating ourselves, then we do not also have to accept anyone else's rating of us as a human being?' he asks.

Dr Jim agrees. 'If we truly accept ourselves as human beings, then it would make no sense to allow others to rate us.' He adds that, from a grief perspective, crying is, and will continue to be, a normal emotional response for Peter and indeed the majority of those who find themselves in such situations.

Peter vows to cease playing the rating game with himself or through others.

On subsequent visits, Dr Jim challenges his two remaining demands. The first related to his demand that 'he must now be left alone and lonely'. Was this absolute demand rational or irrational? Peter agrees on reflection that it was irrational as he had no 'control' over what might or might not happen in the years to come. They agree that he would prefer not to be left alone and lonely, but that this was out of his control. Following discussion, Peter accepts that it is completely unrealistic to demand 100 per cent certainty about this or indeed anything in life. To teach him how to challenge this demand, Dr Jim suggests performing the Coin Exercise detailed on page 56.

They also discuss whether Peter would benefit from researching and involving himself in some new community and social events, hobbies and other engagements. Peter agrees to research this further as a way to head off his feeling of loneliness.

Finally, they progress to challenging his ingrained belief that 'life should be fair' and that 'he must be treated fairly'. Peter, much to his chagrin, learns that 'life was not fair and never would be' as they discuss the reality that 'life is just life' and exceedingly random in its distribution of loss, trauma and other slings and arrows that it throws at us. He learns to drop the grudge he has against life, in order to progress further towards emotional healing.

Within six to twelve months, Peter has at last begun to emotionally self-heal. He now accepts the pain, sadness and vagaries of grief, no longer demanding that they disappear. He has come to regard them as the price that he is paying for the joy and love that Jane and himself had experienced in their marriage.

He has also developed unconditional self-acceptance and is increasingly comfortable in his own skin. He no longer cares or feels concern about how others view him. With Dr Jim's assistance, he has begun the difficult process of picking up the shattered pieces of his life and reintegrating himself back into the community.

Peter is now a regular member of the local Mensheds group, where men – often unemployed, retired or widowed – come together to become involved in practical community projects as a way of maintaining their mental health. He has found consolation in sharing his grief experiences with new members encountering similar losses. He has taken up pitch and putt, dancing and a host of other activities which keep him both busy and mentally healthy. He has developed a network of both male and female companions which prevents him from feeling alone or isolated. He now accepts and teaches others that life is neither fair, certain or free of pain and discomfort.

A year later, he admits to Dr Jim, 'I now realize that I will never stop grieving or thinking about or crying about losing Jane, but am learning how to adapt and change to the new life which her loss has created. But do you know what? I'm now OK with both of these realities.'

His reply was simple.

'Well, Peter, we call that emotional healing.'

12. Coping With The Death Of A Parent

It is the natural order of life that somewhere on the journey, you will lose, or will already have lost, one or other parent to illness, old age or trauma. Here we will focus primarily on the grief process of the adult who loses a parent. The experience of losing a parent in childhood is subtly different from the grief experiences of the adult, especially in the case of younger children. The experiences of the adolescent (even though still considered as children up to the age of eighteen) mirror more closely those of the adult, especially in the later teens, and some of the messages of this chapter may be of assistance to them. It would not be possible to cover the subject of losing a parent as a child in the detail which it deserves in this chapter, but I have recommended some relevant specialist books in the bibliography.

How to Manage the Loss of a Parent

It is important to recognise that each one us loses a 'different' parent and this explains the variety of grief reactions in a family. Each child and adult will have a different relationship with their mother and father. This relationship, in turn, will depend on the individual personality of both parents and child, their place in the family, whether they are closer automatically to one or other parent, and especially what memories have been built up, in their emotional mind, around that parent. It is a sad reality that just because we love our parents or vice versa, it does not inevitably follow that we will like or be close to them as we become adults and build our own lives.

The importance of this insight cannot be overestimated when it comes to losing a parent. Some may find themselves completely distraught and struggling to cope with both the emotional fallout and the changes which their parent's death will introduce into their life. For others, there may be some emotional distress, but of a lesser nature as the relationship between you and your parent may not have been as close. I have even encountered situations where an adult offspring seeks assistance as they feel guilty at not feeling emotionally distressed at their passing.

There are therefore no hard and fast rules as to how best to emotionally grieve following the loss of a parent. There are too many variables in how each one of us will view their passing and therefore multiple different emotional expressions of the grief process. Apart from coping with the emotional aspects of losing your parent, there can be some significant adaptations that you may have to make, to cope with the changes that their loss might introduce into your life.

The following insights, observations and suggestions may assist you in coping with the loss of a parent.

1. There is no 'time limit' on how long you will grieve for them.
2. It is normal to break down, cry or feel sad every time there is a festive holiday or birthday, even years later.

3. There can often be a rush to 'clear out' special belongings that belonged to the parent who has died. Keep them until you feel the time has come to move them onwards.

4. Never fall into the trap of comparing your reaction to the loss of a parent to that of other siblings. This can lead you into dark places. Do not fall into the trap of being hurt, angry or frustrated if your siblings or other relatives do not seem to be showing signs of being as sad or distressed as you. Remember that each one of us is unique, as are our individual relationships or bonds with the parent who has died.

5. There is a different feel to the loss of the first parent as opposed to the second. For some, the former may be your first real experience with the reality of grief and the powerful emotions that can accompany it. When the second parent dies, there can be a strange sense of dislocation as it dawns on you that you are next in line. This may lead you on some occasions to challenge the meaning of your own life. This uncertainty can add to the different emotions and difficulties that their death brings into your world.

6. One of the commonest negative emotions which can plague you following parental loss is that of guilt. This can be present for a variety of reasons. This may relate to issues such as not visiting them sufficiently, having differences which were unresolved prior to the death, not spotting the warning signs of some illness or condition and so on.

7. You may experience other unhealthy emotions such as depression (if you come to believe, for example, that you are 'abnormal' as you are not 'over' your sadness); or

anger at other siblings or medical or nursing professionals if you believe that they did not do enough for your
loved one.

8. If you find yourself becoming distressed that you are not
    grieving as much as other siblings, it is important to em-
    phasize that this may be absolutely normal for you. The
    reality, as we have discussed, is that you will only grieve
    as a human being in proportion to the intensity and
    closeness of the relationship that you have had with the
    person in question. Just because that person happens to
    be a parent does not change this reality.

9. One frequently overlooked change that you may expe-
    rience is where one parent dies and the other is now
    increasingly dependent on you and other siblings either
    for practical or emotional support. This can become an
    increasing issue if there are some chronic physical or
    cognitive conditions present in the surviving parent.

10. Another sad but unfortunately increasingly common
    situation that I have encountered over the decades is
    where a parent dies and there are inter-sibling feuds over
    houses, land, money or wills. You may be grieving badly
    over the loss of your parent, but find yourself caught up
    in this quagmire at the same time.

11. There can also be a maze of legal, financial and other
    tasks to be carried out following the death of your
    parent and this too can be quite a daunting and, in some
    cases, distressing task to carry out. Once again, seek out
    as much professional and family advice and support to
    manage this change.

12. Another often overlooked but important change often
    occurs when the second parent dies. Most families or

groups of siblings find that the presence of the final parent, perhaps living in the house where all of them were reared, keeps the family unit intact, even if siblings are scattered. There is a common denominator keeping them all together. When the final parent dies, especially if it is the mother, this can lead to a splintering of this family unit, with all going their separate ways and only meeting up occasionally.

Claire's Story

Claire has been struggling emotionally since the death of her mother Mary, eighteen months previously. Claire is in her mid-forties, married to Simon, with two children, now in their early teens, and is also a successful businesswoman who is always 'busy'. The death of her mum rekindled emotional memories of the death of her dad, two years previously, with whom she had a special relationship. She had blocked out everything to do with his death and threw herself into a frenzy of work as a coping mechanism. Her mum's sudden death from a heart attack devastated her, even though they had never been especially close.

She attends Dr Jim, seeking some coping strategies. He offers to teach her some CBT techniques to do just that. They decide to use Mary's death as the trigger.

'And how did this make you feel emotionally?' asks Dr Jim.

Claire admits, 'I was surprised at the depths of both sadness and emotional pain I have been encountering since her death, as I was always less attached to my mum, whereas I adored my dad.'

She also admits to feelings of depression, guilt, frustration and, surprisingly, shame. Dr Jim notes that her feelings of sadness and emotional pain could also be the result of a retriggering of such emotions following the death of her dad, which she had sub-merged by trying to stay busy.

'Now, what was your behavioural response to these emotions?' asks Dr Jim. 'What did you do when you felt like this?'

Claire reveals a long history of unhealthy behaviours, such as withdrawing socially, trying to avoid talking about her death to other siblings or friends, ruminating about her failures in relation to her interactions with her mum, eating poorly and losing some weight, drinking too much and, when on her own, breaking down and sobbing uncontrollably.

'And how did these emotions make you feel physically?' asks Dr Jim.

'I felt so tired and demotivated,' she answers. 'Struggling all of the time with sleep and appetite, with constant headaches and my stomach in knots all of the time.'

'What was it about Mary's death that caused you to feel so much sadness and emotional pain?' asks Dr Jim.

'That she is gone from my life and that I won't be able to see either her or my dad again in this life,' she replies.

'And what was it about her death that caused you to feel de-pressed?' asks Dr Jim.

'I feel such a wimp,' Claire replies. 'Other people at work lose parents and seem to handle it well. There must be something wrong with me that I'm not coping. I can't believe that I am still breaking down crying, eighteen months after the death of my mum.'

'And what about her death made you feel guilty?' Dr Jim asks.

'Because I made myself keep busy after Dad's death,' she explains. 'I didn't visit her regularly enough and even kept telephone contact to a minimum. We never really got on and she was forever criticiz-ing how I was rearing the children. If I had been visiting her on a regular basis, I might have picked up some evidence that she was unwell from a heart point of view and prevented her from dying.'

'And shame?' Dr Jim asks.

'I believed that others, especially at work and close friends, could see how poorly I was coping,' she explains, 'and they must have assumed that I was either weak or weird as a result.'

'Let's examine what irrational beliefs were triggered by your mum's death and the inferences you assigned to it,' says Dr Jim.

With Dr Jim's assistance, Claire decides that it was rational, human and healthy to mourn the loss of both her mum and her dad but that they needed to have a discussion about the grief process. Dr Jim promises to elaborate on this further later.

They decide that her belief in relation to her emotion of depression was that because she had not 'got over' her sadness and grief she was weak and weird. In relation to her emotion of guilt they agreed that it was because she felt she should have been able to prevent her mum dying from a heart attack by visiting her frequently.

In relation to her emotion of shame, her demand was that she must accept the harsh judgements of others who were noticing that she was struggling to come to terms with her loss.

They add this information to Claire's ABC:

A – Activating Event:
- Trigger: Mary's death from a sudden heart attack
- Inference/danger: that I will never see my mum or dad again in this life; I am also losing any opportunities to share experiences relating to self or children with them; because I have not got over the deaths of my parents, I am weak and weird; perhaps if I had visited my mother regularly, I might have picked up evidence of an underlying

heart condition and prevented her death; others might notice that I am not coping with my grief and judge me accordingly.

B – Belief/Demands:

- 'My parents are gone, and I will never see them again in this life.' 'Because I have not "got over" my grief and sadness, I am weak and weird.' 'I should have been able to prevent my mother dying from a heart attack by visiting her frequently.' 'People will judge me harshly and I must accept their negative judgements.'

C – Consequences:

- Emotional reactions: sadness; emotional pain; depression; guilt and shame
- Physical reactions: fatigue; sleep difficulties; lack of motivation; tension headaches and stomach in knots
- Behaviour: spending increasing time on her own; withdrawing socially; drinking excessively; struggling to eat normally; ruminating obsessively about how she had treated her mum.

Dr Jim then begins to challenge her behaviours, asking if they are in any way assisting her in relation to her current situation. Claire admits that her increasing habits of social isolation and excessive drinking, together with her poor diet, are creating physical and mental-health difficulties in her life. She promises to make changes.

Dr Jim then challenges Claire's beliefs and demands. They begin with a major discussion on the whole grief process. How the pain and sadness is not time-limited but could continue, coming and going in waves, and for some people would stay with them for life. How the journey of grief is different for each person.

Claire now realizes that the intense sadness, allied to bouts of crying and intense emotional pain, are a normal part of the grief process.

They also discussed how the death of her mum had triggered the release of buried emotions relating to the death of her dad.

'This is common,' Dr Jim explains. 'Sometimes the pain and sadness are too great following the loss of someone extremely close to us, and our mind just shuts these emotions down. But inevitably they will resurface at some stage and it can often be the death of another loved one which triggers them.

'Now, let's explore your belief that because you have not got over your sadness and grief, you are weak and weird. Do you believe that this is rational or irrational?'

Claire admits that, following their discussion on the grief process, this was probably irrational in relation to this situation.

'But can a human being be described as weak or weird or abnormal to begin with?' asks Dr Jim.

Following a lively conversation about the world of personal self-rating, Claire finally admits that human beings cannot be described in such a manner, but that their behaviour and skills and talents can be. They discuss the importance of Unconditional Self-Acceptance and how to achieve it. Claire finds herself feeling quite emotional as she thinks about the freedom which this could bring into her life as she has spent years playing the rating game.

'And what about your belief that others would judge you because you did not seem to be coping with your grief?' Dr Jim asks.

Claire, following on from their discussion on rating, accepts that this, too, is irrational. 'What you are saying is that I do not have to accept other people's rating or judgement of me as a person,' she ventures, and Dr Jim agrees.

This leads to a discussion on how poorly understood the grief process is, particularly amongst those who had yet to experience a serious loss in their lives.

Dr Jim then tackles the major irrational belief which underlies Claire's emotion of guilt.

'Do you believe that your demand that you should have been able to prevent your mother dying from a heart attack by visiting her frequently is rational or irrational?' he asks.

Claire really struggles with this. 'But is this not rational?' she protests. 'If I had been visiting more often, surely I would have picked up warning signs that she was unwell and prevented her death?'

'Do you have the ability to see into the future?' Dr Jim asks.

Claire admits she does not. 'Are you suggesting,' she says, 'that it is unreasonable for me to have known what was going to happen to my mum and therefore I couldn't have prevented it?'

Dr Jim agrees, 'All of us in life are constantly making decisions and some will work out and others will not. You can only make decisions, such as how often to visit your mum, with whom you had a strained relationship, based on the information you have at that time and the emotional state you are in when making the decision.'

This was a life-changing insight for Claire as she accepts that she could not possibly have known that her mum had an underlying cardiac illness. She understands that her decision to visit less frequently was based on both her lack of knowledge about this and her longstanding difficulties relationship-wise with her. She feels as if a weight has been lifted off her shoulders.

Six months later, Claire is coping better with both carrying her heavy burden of sadness and emotional pain, and with adapting to the many changes which the death of both of her parents has introduced into her life. She now understands and accepts that emotions such as sadness and emotional pain would come and go, for the rest of her life, but that this too is OK.

She has re-engaged with many of her friends, is back to her normal weight, exercising and careful with alcohol. She no longer worries about the occasional periods of crying when something reminds her especially of her dad and ceases to care what others might think about seeing her in this state. She has become increasingly self-accepting of herself and is teaching this skill to her children. Claire's healing process is well under way.

13. Coping With The Death Of A Child

There can be few greater traumas than the loss of a child. It is a savage blow, which can emotionally tear us asunder. It is unnatural for a parent to be looking at the body of their child and not the other way around. The grief process which ensues can be complex, emotionally painful and can seriously challenge your capacity to survive and adapt.

This chapter explores how to 'survive' the harsh, bleak landscape of grief, following on from losing a child. It is a life-changing event. I have been privileged to walk alongside some wonderful people on this survival journey and have shared the grief experiences of those who have lost children to illness, accidents, suicide, miscarriages, neonatal deaths and other causes.

They have taught me the wisdom of using the word 'survival' to describe the reality of the grief process which follows such a loss. We simply never 'get over' such a loss. It is too profound, too raw, too devastating for our emotional minds to ever come to terms with. But we *can* learn to survive, and survive we must, for ourselves and for those around us.

In life, we cope because we must, not because we want to. There are few other occasions in life where this statement will challenge us as much as following the death of a child.

It is important to clarify what we mean on these pages by the word 'child'. As parents, no matter what age our offspring are, from small children to young or mature adults, we will always consider them as our 'child'. For the purposes of this chapter, however, we are discussing here the death of a child or young person up to the age of thirty.

It is often assumed that it is the mother who suffers most from the loss of a child. Mothers, of course, struggle greatly when grieving a child. Not only with intense sadness and emotional pain, but with unhealthy emotions such as guilt. All mothers instinctively believe that they should be able to protect and guard their offspring from danger and that if their child dies prematurely, they have somehow let them down. But grieving fathers too can suffer deeply and often silently in the background, especially if the child dies due to suicide or trauma. Fathers may also believe that they have failed in their duty to protect their offspring and this can lead to feeling guilty and depressed. In my personal experience, fathers can be the silent victims of grief after a child dies, as this tragedy unfolds with the majority of attention being diverted towards the mother.

If you have experienced such a devastating loss either recently or in the past, the following observations and advice given may be of assistance.

How to Cope Emotionally with the Death of a Child

Your initial emotional state is going to be numbness as your body and mind tries desperately to deal with the shock you have been dealt. This is usually followed by levels of sadness and emotional pain that are simply impossible to describe or cope with, due to their raw intensity and depth. Losing a child tears a hole in your heart that will simply never be filled. The pain you are feeling can only be described by those who have felt it, and even then with difficulty.

Alongside this pain usually comes a plethora of other negative emotions such as intense anger, depression, guilt and hurt. Guilt and anger will often try to dominate and prevent you from experiencing the true extent of your sadness and loss, which can be unbearable.

There is also the second dimension of the grief process for you to cope with. When a child dies, nobody in that home is ever going to be the same again. As was once described to me, the family unit is like a ring. If you remove a portion of the ring, then the circle, representing the family unit, is irrevocably broken. The make-up of the family unit is for ever altered, as are the relationships between parents and remaining siblings.

You will be battling the silence where the person's presence and voice are gone, as are all your hopes and dreams for them. For you have lost what they might have become, just as much as the child itself. You must adapt to the new situation, and to a new you, neither of which will ever be the same again.

There is little that I can do to ease your pain and distress or prepare you for the major life changes which will occur if you have experienced the loss of a child.

Here are some emotional 'survival tips', however, that parents have shared with me, together with some insights and practical advice that I have gleaned from experience.

1. Everything that we discussed in chapter nine on how to cope with the sadness and emotional pain is especially true if you have lost a child and I refer you back to that

section. Remember that this process is not time-limited. You may never find the pain and sadness getting any easier, but you will reach a time where you are better able to cope with and carry the load.

2. It is routine that will save you from feeling as if you are going mad with the sadness of grief, especially in the year following the loss of your child. In the beginning, the simplest of tasks may seem insurmountable and you will often feel like giving up. Getting out of bed, showering, eating, doing normal domestic chores, going through the motions at work are all part of a subtle package of activities that will help you to survive this most painful of times. Cling to routine and let it soothe and support you.

3. There is no right or wrong way to emotionally grieve such a loss – there is simply your way. Spend as much time as you need in the rubble of your grief. Only begin to put your life back together when you feel ready to do so, not when someone else feels it is appropriate.

4. It is important to deal with the powerful emotions of guilt and anger but also depression, which may form a significant portion of your emotional distress. Guilt and anger are constant companions to parents who have lost a child, with the latter especially damaging to themselves as well as others. If you can relate to these emotions, then you will find helpful advice on pages 113–125 and 149–166.

5. There may be specific places where you feel the presence of your child and others where you may not. For some it may be the cemetery. For others it is often the child's bedroom or treasured possessions that may bring them closer. Decide what works for you, even if such places trigger powerful emotions of sadness and copious tears.

Mothers often find the bedroom of the dead child a place where they can sense the presence of their loved one. This may be comforting at times, and distressing at others, so pay attention to how you are feeling.

6. You may feel the need to hide your true feelings from your remaining children and, on occasions, your partner, believing that this will protect them from the painful emotions that you are experiencing, and not wanting to be another burden on them. In my experience, men are especially likely to fall into this trap, not wanting to upset their wives, partners or remaining children.

   The reality is that each surviving member of the family who has lost a child, whether mother, father or siblings, will mourn the loss in their own unique manner. By not allowing your family members to witness your grief, they may feel that they are not coping or should not be showing their distress in front of you, which is unhealthy for both parties. In order for you all to heal emotionally, I urge you to allow other family members to see you crying and struggling, and they too will share their emotions with you.

7. A significant issue for both parents but especially the mum is how to deal with the possessions and room of the dead child. Parents may become distressed as other siblings or close friends push to clear out the room or discard such possessions. My advice is to hold on to these until you have reached a point where you are coping better with the sadness and pain and believe it is time to intervene further. Trust that you will know when to begin letting go of these possessions.

8. Sometimes there can be such a preoccupation with grieving

for the child who is dead that you forget those children who have survived. They may feel hurt or rejected if you forget to take care of their needs and emotional difficulties, due to a preoccupation with the child who has died. Remember they are the future, and make an effort, even in your own pain, to maintain your relationships with them.

When Your Child Dies by Suicide

Those left behind in the wake of a suicide are sometimes called 'suicide survivors'. This confusing term suggests that the person 'survived' the attempt but in practice relates to the person or persons left behind following their death. It is no coincidence that the term 'survivor' is used here as a description, for 'survival' is the best that most parents can aim for, in the months and years that follow losing their child in such a manner. There is considerable interest in the concept of suicide bereavement counselling, with evidence from research that lives can be saved by assisting those left behind to develop better coping mechanisms. There is also a higher incidence following such suicides of related physical symptoms such as cardiovascular incidents, especially heart attacks, some of which may prove fatal. There is also an increased risk of depression and, worryingly, suicide itself, as a coping mechanism to deal with the loss of a loved one.

Surviving parents form an especially high-risk group for self-harm or suicide, due to a combination of guilt, self-loathing, intense sadness, depression and a longing to be with the person who has died.

There are several observations and insights that parents who have lost children to suicide have shared with me, which you may find helpful:

1. Many parents mention the emotion of shame, which hangs around them and their families, like a miasma or cloak. The society name for this is 'stigma', but the reality is that many parents do believe that they are being judged negatively for not protecting their child.

2. They also discuss the special quality of loneliness which follows in the wake of the death of their child. This loneliness is not just related to the absence of the child they loved, but to the uniqueness of the experience for the parents who survive. Only parents who have experienced such a loss could come even close to understanding the depth of emotions unleashed and the enormity of the emotional pain experienced.

3. Some parents describe how the intense sadness and pain they have experienced comes in waves which threaten to overwhelm them. How this pain and sadness never leaves. How they feel as if they are going mad. How they believe that they will never be the same again. How they fear their lives will always be filled with pain. Some parents worry that festival periods and birthdays may become an ordeal to be endured rather than joyous occasions, reminding them of the way life used to be when their child was alive. My message of hope is that over time you will begin to adjust and adapt to your new situation. Joy and laughter will once again be part of such occasions, even if tinged with sadness as you remember your loved one. Some parents have shared with me that they have kept up traditions which their loved ones would have been involved with at such times, and sense their presence more as a result, and find this quite comforting. Others find it helpful at such occasions to

set a place at the table for the loved one who has died as it assists them to sense that their loved one is present and sharing the occasion with them. You must find what works for you and your family at such times. You cannot change what has happened, but you can learn to adapt to the changed situation which their loss has introduced into your life.

4.   Some parents may become increasingly religious or spiritual, for example, whilst others may become increasingly agnostic. If the former, then hopefully this will bring some solace and meaning into your life as you grieve, as you may look forward to meeting them in another existence and time. Your belief may also inspire you to become actively involved in assisting those struggling with their mental health. If the latter, where you may not believe that you will see your child again in another life, it is equally important that you discover meaning and purpose following on from such a loss. I have known parents who have thrown themselves into providing services for those who are struggling with their mental health and for whom suicide has become an option. Others have decided to give their time and effort to assisting sporting or other activities which would improve the mental health and wellbeing of young people. You must find your own road. It is so important to find meaning as it is the engine which drives us on to continue positively with our lives, despite the tragedy which has struck us. I sometimes call this 'healing through meaning'.

5.   It is impossible to explain just how guilty the majority of parents feel that they somehow failed to prevent the

death, even if they had no sense that their child was so distressed. Deep down, these parents know it is irrational, but they still cling on to this unhealthy emotion.

6. Another unspoken thought relates to the intensity of the desire to be with the child who has died. This can be intensely powerful for mothers but also for some fathers who are struggling with the loss. I have known situations where only the presence of other children has kept a parent from taking their own life. Therefore it is essential to have this discussion as to how best to cope with such a loss.

7. Some parents talk of 'time standing still' in relation to the child who has died. They describe it as if the child is now frozen in time at the age at which they died. It may be a particular photograph that in their minds will always be how they remember them. It is why some mothers are unable to change or move anything in the bedroom of the child or get rid of their clothes because they can still smell their presence.

8. Mothers especially discuss how the fabric of their families will never be the same again. How their lives and hearts are broken into small pieces and that these pieces cannot ever be 'glued together' again. How everything has changed forever. This insight is important as you may be feeling like this at this moment in time. You are not alone. I have never met a mother who did not feel like this. For emotional healing to occur, you will have to accept that this is one of the changes which the loss of your child is going to introduce into your heart as well as your home. If I can find meaning by ensuring that you are there for the other important people in your life,

such as your partner or other children, you will find it so much easier to cope. This insight will assist you to emotionally self-heal. Think of it as if a precious item of porcelain has broken into pieces, with one of those pieces shattered completely. You can gradually put together the pieces which remain to make a new, if incomplete, version of what you have lost. It may not be perfect, but over time, you will learn to accept what is created anew.

9. Another common admission is the difficulties that parents, especially men, experience when meeting friends and acquaintances, subsequent to the suicide of their child. These conversations can be incredibly hard for all parties. It is hard not to break down into tears on some occasions, and many parents will now see themselves as 'different' because of their experience, in the eyes of those they meet. How often they wish that the conversation could revert to normal daily topics rather than discussing their pain and sadness. This is an important insight which you may find helpful. Firstly, you are not alone if experiencing such social interactions. Secondly, it is the situation which is abnormal, not you, so be kind to yourself and stop rating and judging yourself as 'abnormal' or 'different'. Finally, do not be afraid to say to friends or acquaintances that you are struggling with your loss if you are crying in their presence.

10. Apart from the intensity of the grief process, the one common denominator that unites most parents who have experienced this loss is their question as to 'why' their child made this decision. I have seen this question almost destroy some parents as they remain locked in a world

of unhealthy negative emotions such as guilt, anger and depression as they are unable to uncover an answer that allows them to emotionally heal. My first message to such parents is that this question in my experience has the capacity to destroy your peace of mind and inner calm. It is closely related in my clinical experience with the emotion of guilt, which we have explored in some detail. Sometimes there may be an obvious answer, such as the child was suffering from some significant mental illness. But in a significant number of cases, the reasons underlying their action are more likely to remain hidden or uncertain. My own explanation to parents is that we usually decide to take our own lives when we encounter some problem (either a life-crisis situation, mental illness or both combined) which we deem impossible to resolve by any other means. My second message is that constantly tormenting yourself in trying to answer a question which may have no obvious answer, is only going to increase your emotional distress. For emotional healing to occur, you will have to accept that sometimes human beings make such decisions, for whatever reasons, and that we must learn to accept that this is a reality and that no amount of introspection will change that reality. My third message is that focusing solely on this question will tend to block you in dealing with the sadness and emotional pain which are the core essence of grief when your child dies by suicide. If you can learn to accept these three messages and absorb them into your psyche, then emotional healing will follow.

We have already discussed in detail some coping mechanisms to deal with the emotional and change aspects of losing a child and all this information is equally applicable to the death of a child through suicide. Frequently, however, the intensity of the experience and the difficulties involved in coping with the changes which arise following such a death may require professional or counselling assistance. Some parents find this helpful, others not. In my experience, men often wish to handle matters themselves as they find the subject too difficult and painful to share with anyone else. I believe that men are better off engaging with other fathers who have endured a similar experience and who can share and empathise with each other. In a moment we will be visiting with Chris and see how he learned to 'survive' his loss. Before that, here are a few insights that may be of assistance.

1. Life will never be the same and neither will you. Try to accept this reality from the outset and it will make matters a little easier.

2. There is often no clear answer as to 'why' your child has made the decision and it is easier to just accept this from the onset. Even if you did know why, ask if it would really assist you in dealing with the sadness and pain? My own belief is that your major challenge is learning, over time, how to manage and carry the burden of your loss and that answering this question doesn't really change that reality.

3. Remember that your child did not die by suicide to hurt you but to cope with some underlying emotional distress which they believed could not be managed in any other way, even if this latter is untrue. When human beings become emotionally distressed, it is easy for rational logic to go out the window.

4. There are two things that can keep us alive, whilst floating and attempting to survive on the turbulent seas of

grief following the death of a child to suicide. The first is clinging on to routine, no matter how bad things get. The second relates to the presence in your life of other people you love and who love you. It is the latter that really matters in life, the rest is irrelevant.

Chris's Story

Chris is referred to see Dr Jim by his family doctor following a serious suicide attempt. His story echoes the experiences of many parents.

Chris was a university lecturer and married to Emma, a primary school teacher. They had three children aged between twenty-two and fifteen, and a great relationship with sounds of joy, laughter and fun regularly permeating the house. Then, on a bleak October day, tragedy arrived. Their son Michael unexpectedly and without prior warning took his own life. Seemingly happy with the business-degree course which he had been taking in college, he had been in a long-standing relationship with Susan since his late teens. He left no suicide note or explanation as to why he had taken the decision he did. Even more traumatically for Chris, he was the one who found the body in the shed at the back of their house.

The following two years were a nightmare time for the couple. Both were devastated, as were the two remaining siblings, all of them feeling guilty that they had somehow missed something that might have prevented the tragedy. They received bereavement counselling, but Chris did not find it of assistance, and terminated the sessions.

Chris and Emma handled their grief differently. Emma took solace in her strong faith but still found herself constantly overwhelmed by bouts of intense sadness and crying. She insisted that

Michael's bedroom and clothes were left untouched, finding peace and a sense of his presence in the room. She had not revealed to Chris how one evening, when she was sitting crying in his room, Michael had appeared at the end of the bed, smiling at her before slowly disappearing. She visited his grave regularly, finding some solace there. Her remaining son and daughter's mental health became a primary concern. She became completely overprotective, anxious that nothing would happen to them. She also became increasingly concerned about Chris, who had retreated into his own shell, refusing to even discuss Michael's death, and behaving as if he wanted to block it all out. There were times, as she admitted to her mum, when she believed that she was losing him. She enlisted the assistance of her mum, close friends and a bereavement counsellor in her battle to cope with the unbearable loss of her son.

Chris, too, was overwhelmed with powerful negative emotions. He simply couldn't bear the waves of sadness and emotional pain that were present when he woke up in the morning and stayed with him like a cloud during the daytime, even disturbing his sleep. His dreams were of Michael stretching out his hands, beseeching him for help, with Chris frantically trying to reach him. But no matter how hard he tried, in this dream Michael always seemed to be moving further away.

Alongside his unbearable pain came intense emotions of guilt, anger, hurt, shame and depression. He struggled at work, became broody, prickly and withdrawn at home, finding solace increasingly with alcohol. Of increasing concern to both partners, he was struggling to relate to Emma, who was coping with her grief through prayer, counselling and focusing on her remaining children.

Chris had always been agnostic in his belief systems, finding meaning through his work and family. Now that meaning had been blown away by Michael's death. He found himself increasingly railing at life and the injustice of it all. The idea of a 'loving' God who had snatched his child away so pitilessly, was, in his eyes, laughable. Michael was gone and was never coming back in this world or any other, and anyone who thought otherwise was much to be pitied.

But it was the guilt and shame that were eating him up inside. How could he have missed the signs that something was wrong? What must others think of him as a father who could not protect his own son? What followed were feelings of depression and self-loathing that dragged him down, into the dark world of ruminatory, suicidal thoughts. It was a short step, fuelled by alcohol, to his suicide attempt. He hated doing it to Emma and his two children, but couldn't cope with the thoughts in his head and the pain that he believed would follow him indefinitely. He reasoned that they too would be better off without him. Wasn't he a failure anyway?

He survived the attempt, waking up in a hospital bed, initially angry that he had been unsuccessful but then overwhelmed by the reactions of Emma, his children, parents and siblings. Their love and palpable distress shocked him out of the deadly downwards spiral which Michael's suicide had initiated. Following some discussions with a self-harm liaison nurse and his family doctor, Chris agreed to attend Dr Jim.

Dr Jim listens empathetically to Chris as he pours out the story of how he had been struggling to come to terms with the sadness and pain. How he was wracked with guilt and shame. How he felt that he had let everyone down, especially Emma, by his behaviour since Michael had died and now by his suicide attempt. Dr Jim explains that it was unsurprising that Chris had been struggling.

'It is hard enough to cope when someone close to us dies,' he says, 'but when it is your own child and they have died by suicide, the grief process which follows can be almost unbearable. It is hard for someone who has not experienced such a loss to comprehend the suffering and pain that this can bring into the life of the individual person and everyone else in the family affected.'

This leads into a fruitful discussion on the grief process and how it introduces a plethora of negative emotions such as sadness and guilt and how Michael's death would fundamentally change Chris and his family's lives for ever.

'You cannot change this reality,' Dr Jim explains, 'but we can explore whether changing your thinking and behaviours following such a loss might allow you to cope better and develop strategies to survive in the new world you find yourself inhabiting.'

Chris inquires whether he could provide him with such coping strategies, and Dr Jim agrees to explore some CBT techniques to do just that. He explains about rational and irrational beliefs and lays out the ABC concepts, explaining how they will employ this system to locate and manage his irrational beliefs. They decide to use Michael's death as the trigger.

'And how did this make you feel emotionally?' asks Dr Jim.

Chris admits that following the death and the initial period of shock and numbness which followed, he had experienced intense sadness and deep-seated emotional pain.

'It never left me,' he explains. 'I was constantly crying inside but blocked out any public display of tears. Emma was crying enough tears for both of us and I didn't want to upset her or the other kids any further as they were already struggling. Anyway, real men don't cry.'

On further probing, Chris admits to feelings of guilt, anger, shame and depression, but 'guilt' in his own words was the emotion that brought him to his knees.

'What were your behavioural responses to these emotions?' asks Dr Jim. 'What did you do when you felt like this?'

This opens up a Pandora's box of unhealthy behaviours such as withdrawing from Emma, becoming irritable and moody, losing interest in almost everything at work and domestically, drinking excessively, struggling with eating, sleeping and maintaining exercise, constantly ruminating and brooding about what signs he had missed in Michael, avoiding other people, refusing to attend further counselling and finally a suicide attempt.

'None of these worked so well,' he admits.

He also adds, on questioning, that physically he had constant fatigue, lack of motivation, had lost weight, struggled with cognition and found sleep impossible.

They decide to add this information to Chris's ABC:

A – Activating Event:
- Trigger: Michael's death by suicide
- Inference/danger:

B – Belief/Demands:

C – Consequences:
- Emotional reactions: sadness; emotional pain; guilt; anger; shame and depression
- Physical reactions: fatigue; sleep difficulties; lack of motivation; poor cognition
- Behaviour: becomes irritable and moody; withdraws emotionally from Emma; drinking excessively; loses interest in work and domestically; struggles with diet, exercise and sleep; constantly ruminates and broods

about what he had missed in relation to Michael's pre-suicide state; self-harm attempt.

Dr Jim then began to explore what inferences that Chris had taken from the death of Michael that led him to experience the mixture of emotions described. He asks Chris: 'What was it about Michael's death that caused you to feel so much sadness and emotional pain?'

'That's easy to answer,' replies Chris. 'He's gone, and I am never going to see him again. We had such a wonderful relationship and I felt so close to him. When he was a child, we did everything together. He was the eldest, so there was that special bond there from the beginning. I love them all to bits, but he was most like me, whilst the others take after Emma.'

On further probing he admits, 'I am a complete agnostic so don't even have the luxury of believing that I might see him in another guise or world'.

He then breaks down crying, 'I just can't believe he is gone. What we had between us was so special. He was never off the phone, and always seemed so happy and content with life.'

He proceeds to show Dr Jim a photo of Michael, 'I just can't accept that I will never see his lovely smile again'.

He also admits how he envies Emma that she can still sense his presence in his bedroom and at the grave, and for her faith, even if he believes it is pointless.

'I, on the other hand, just feel an emptiness inside. A gnawing ache in my heart which will never be filled.'

Dr Jim empathizes with him on how painful these emotions are and promises to return to them later.

'But what was it about Michael's death by suicide that made you feel so guilty?' he asks.

'I am certain that I missed something,' Chris replies. 'There must have been some obvious signs that he was not himself, or that something was wrong in his life, and yet I never spotted it.'

'And why is that distressing you so much?' Dr Jim asks.

'Because if I had only been more observant, I might have been able to intervene and stop him from destroying his beautiful young life, where he had so much to give,' replies Chris sadly. 'I can never forgive myself for letting him down so badly. I was simply not there for him when he needed me most'.

'What was it about Michael's death by suicide that made you feel angry?' Dr Jim asks.

'I was angry with Michael for not coming to me and letting me know that he was struggling,' replies Chris. 'Instead he did what he did, which leaves me, his mum and his siblings to carry the burden of his loss.'

'And ashamed?' asks Dr Jim.

'What must other people have thought of me?' replies Chris. 'It is the job of a father to protect his child and I failed miserably. I am a college lecturer, so they would assume that I would notice if a young person was struggling or not. I know they must have judged me as useless and a failure.'

'And depressed?' asks Dr Jim.

'Once again, that is easy to answer,' replies Chris. 'I cannot describe just how much self-loathing there has been. I believed that I was useless, weak, a failure, a worthless father, husband and human being.'

'Let's examine, finally, what irrational beliefs were triggered by Michael's death and the inferences you assigned to it,' says Dr Jim. 'This usually takes the form of some absolute demands you were making about the trigger, which in this case was his death.'

With Dr Jim's assistance, Chris agrees that it was rational, human and healthy to mourn the loss of his son but that they needed to have a discussion as to what the normal course of such a loss would look like. Dr Jim promises to talk about this later.

They then explore other irrational beliefs and demands he was making about Michael's death. They begin by exploring his demand in relation to his emotion of guilt, the emotion which had plagued him from the beginning of his grief journey. Following discussion, they agree that his demand was 'that he should have known that Michael was significantly emotionally distressed and should have been able to prevent his dying by suicide'. In relation to his emotion of shame, they decide that 'other people had judged him negatively, as unable to protect Michael and that he must accept their judgements'. Underlying his bursts of intense anger, they decide that his demand was that 'Michael should have come to him for assistance and should not have taken the action he did and caused so much distress to both Chris and other members of his family'. Behind his depression lay the belief that 'because he had failed Michael, he was useless, a failure and worthless'.

They add this information to complete Chris's ABC:

A – Activating Event:
- Trigger: Michael's death by suicide
- Inference/danger: that Michael is gone and I will never see him again in this world or any other world; the pain I am experiencing will never go away; I had failed to spot any warning signs that Michael was distressed and to prevent him dying by suicide; Michael could have come to me for assistance rather than taking the actions he did; others would believe that I was unable to protect my own son; because I had been unable to prevent Michael

from dying by suicide, I believe that I am a failure and useless.

B – Belief/Demands:

- 'Michael is gone, and I will never see him again.' 'I should have known Michael was emotionally distressed and should have prevented his death.' 'Michael should have come to me for assistance and should not have done what he did.' 'Other people will judge me negatively and I must accept their judgements.' 'Because I was unable to prevent Michael's suicide, I am a failure, useless and worthless.'

C – Consequences:

- Emotional reactions: sadness; emotional pain; guilt; anger; shame and depression
- Physical reactions: fatigue; sleep difficulties; lack of motivation; poor cognition
- Behaviour: becomes irritable and moody; withdraws emotionally from Emma; drinking excessively; loses interest in work and domestically; struggles with diet, exercise and sleep; constantly ruminates and broods about what he had missed in relation to Michael's pre-suicide state; self-harm attempt.

Now that Chris has a better understanding of why he has become so emotionally distressed, he begins, with Dr Jim's assistance, to examine and challenge the thinking and behaviours uncovered.

They begin by Dr Jim challenging his behaviours, as he asks, 'Are these in any way assisting you in relation to your current situation?'

Chris admits that his moodiness and emotional withdrawal from Emma and others, together with his drinking, poor lifestyle habits and constant rumination and brooding, had made matters considerably worse. He was especially upset about his self-harm attempt and the effects that this had on his family.

The real work begins, however, when Dr Jim challenges his beliefs and demands. They start with a major discussion on the whole grief process. How the pain and sadness was not time-limited but would continue, coming and going in waves, and these might stay with him for life. How the journey of grief is different for each person. How the challenge is not only to deal with the raw emotions such as sadness and emotional pain, but also how to adapt to the changes which the loss of a loved one brought into their lives.

'But there are so many times that I feel that I cannot go on,' says Chris. 'How can I face a lifetime of this pain and sadness?'

'But do we really have a choice?' asks Dr Jim. 'Can we just down tools and sit in the middle of the floor and say that I will no longer cope?'

Chris smiles at the absurdity of this. 'I don't think that would work,' he agrees, 'but what is the point of going on?'

Dr Jim challenges this statement. 'You have so many other people who love and rely on you,' he replies.

He then gives Chris the mantra by which he would learn to live: 'I can put up with anything in life, even the death of my son, if it is in my own interest, or in the interests of those I love.'

Chris feels something shifting inside him. 'You are asking me to take my head out of the sand and see how Emma and my two surviving children need and love me, and telling me that I have to find a way to move on, for their sakes.'

Dr Jim agrees, 'It is not going to be easy and only a day by day, week by week approach, allied to the normal daily routines of life, is going to assist you to survive this trauma.'

This leads to a discussion on how it was all about survival, and the tasks of learning how to adapt to the changed life situation which Chris and his family found themselves inhabiting.

'You will never stop mourning the loss of Michael,' explains Dr Jim. 'The pain and sadness will always be there, but you will learn to accept it as a part of your life. The real battle now is to readjust to the new situation that you find yourself in.'

Chris, for the first time since Michael's death, sees a chink of light and a way forward appearing out of the darkness. It will not be easy, but he vows to begin the process for himself and especially for Emma and his two daughters.

On subsequent visits, Dr Jim tackles the irrational beliefs underlying Chris's unhealthy negative emotions, beginning with guilt.

'Do you believe that your demand that you should have known Michael was emotionally distressed and you should have been able to prevent it, is rational or irrational?' he asks.

'Rational,' replies Chris.

'Do you have the ability to see into the future?' Dr Jim asks.

Chris admits he doesn't. 'Are you suggesting,' he asks, 'that it is unreasonable for me to expect to have known that Michael was distressed, unless he disclosed it, and that it was therefore impossible to prevent his suicide?'

Dr Jim agrees and asks, 'When you were Michael's age, would you have discussed such difficulties with your parents?'

Chris admits he would not have.

This leads to a deeper discussion on how we can only do our best to prepare our children for life but cannot protect them from it. How the period from eighteen to twenty-five can be a difficult time for young men, for multiple reasons, and how common it is to hide emotional difficulties from their parents. How sometimes they could become emotionally overwhelmed and see no other path out of their difficulties.

They agree that Chris could spend his life whipping himself emotionally as he would be unable to discover the reason 'why' Michael did what he did. Would it not be easier to accept that Chris had done his best to prepare Michael for life, but that sometimes life takes over, despite our best intentions. Chris vows to try and change his thinking in relation to this belief, as he now realizes how damaging it has been.

In a similar vein, they challenge the demand that lay behind his anger 'that Michael should have come to him and should not have done what he did'. Chris now accepts that Michael was probably trying to protect Emma and himself by not sharing the burden he was carrying with them and forgives him in his heart.

Finally, Dr Jim challenges the two demands that underlie Chris's emotions of shame and depression, namely, that because he had been unable to prevent Michael's suicide 'others would judge him and he must accept their judgement' and that he was 'a failure, useless and worthless'.

This leads to an important discussion where Dr Jim challenges Chris as to whether human beings can be rated or measured or defined in such terms. They also discuss how it was his internal or pathological critic which was trying to convince him that these allegations were true. He introduces Chris to the concept of Unconditional Self-Acceptance, where he would cease rating himself as a person or allowing others to do so, but would accept himself for the special, unique person that he is. How he could only rate his behaviour, and had to accept that in life, he could only do the best he can in this area. How he could not rate himself personally, for example, as a failure but could only rate his behaviour as such, and how the only failure in life was not getting back up and trying again. Chris realises that he has the opportunity to do so with his remaining children and vows to do that. He would also never again see himself as 'worthless' as he now understands that this was simply a form of self-rating or judgement. He also agrees with Dr Jim about not accepting other people's rating of him for the same reasons.

This is a life-changing moment for Chris, and he feels a weight lifted off his shoulders.

Over the months and years that follow, Chris, with the assistance of his wife and Dr Jim, slowly begins to put together the pieces of his life, accepting that it is a 'new life' and that he is a 'changed person' but that too is OK. He still struggles when the waves of sadness and pain hit him suddenly like a buffeting wind and shake him to his core. It is often something small which triggers it, a word, a memory, a smell or a festive occasion. His relationship with Emma deepens and strengthens, as do his relationships with his daughters. Gradually he learns to adjust and adapt to his new world.

Michael will always be there in his heart, as will the pain of the loss of all the times that they could have shared. No longer, however, is he obsessed with questions such as 'why' as he now realizes that this is simply an obstacle in the way of learning how to manage and cope with his loss. Chris and Emma are just 'survivors' and nothing is ever going to change that reality. On one occasion, he shares with Dr Jim how for the first time in several years he noticed the family enjoying themselves and laughing together, despite their continued grief, and how he now accepts that this too is OK. They agree that this is what Michael would have wished for the family he left behind. Dr Jim also adds that this insight is a sure sign that Chris is now on a path of genuine emotional healing.

Conclusion

We began our journey with a promise to assist you in putting your life back together following a bout of significant emotional distress from whatever cause. I hope that you have, in part or fully, achieved this objective and found yourself and your experiences reflected in some of the stories shared here. Perhaps you were living in the world of fear or anxiety, or in the distressing world of self- or other-rating, leading to depression or shame. Perhaps the cause of your distress lay in the darker worlds of hurt, anger or guilt. Perhaps you found yourself existing in the sometimes-bleak landscape of loss, with its intense emotions of sadness and emotional pain.

Whatever the source of your emotional distress, I pray that you have found some peace and inner healing, and have discovered a route out of the turmoil which was blighting your life. If you have gained some insights and skills on the way, such as how to change irrational thinking and unhealthy behavioural patterns, which might make future bouts of emotional distress less burdensome, this is a real bonus. Building your resilience toolkit is an important part of maintaining your emotional healing.

Life is one long emotional rollercoaster, and it is likely that you will find yourself returning regularly to the well of emotional healing found in these pages. The good news is that you now understand how best to tap into this well, which is inside us all.

Emotional healing is all about putting the pieces of your life together again when your emotional world is splintered and broken. It is about becoming whole again. It is about rediscovering who you really are and learning to be at peace with what you find. It is about continuing to apply the lessons learned or insights gained for the rest of your life. It is about learning how to love and accept yourself unconditionally for the wonderful, special, unique person that you are. It is about learning to accept and cope with whatever life throws at you.

The gift of emotional healing is one of the most priceless in life, and I hope it may help you when you need it most.

Dr Harry Barry

BIBLIOGRAPHY

Part One: Emotional Healing

1. What is Emotional Healing?

Barry, H. P. (2009). *Flagging the Therapy: Pathways out of Depression and Anxiety.* Liberties Press Dublin.

Barry, H. P. (2016). *Anxiety and Panic: How to Reshape your Anxious Mind and Brain.* Liberties Press Dublin.

Barry, H. P. (2017). *Emotional Resilience: How to Safeguard your Mental Health.* Orion Spring.

Barry, H. P. (2018). *Self-Acceptance: How to Banish the Self-Esteem Myth, Accept Yourself Unconditionally and Revolutionize your Mental Health.* Orion Spring.

Davidson, R. J. and Begley, S. (2013). *The Emotional Life of your Brain – How to Change the Way you Think, Feel and Live.* Hodder and Stoughton London.

Ellis, A. (1962). *Reason and Emotion in Psychotherapy.* Lyle Stuart New York.

Ellis, A. (1996). *Better, Deeper and More Enduring Brief Therapy. The Rational Emotive Behaviour Therapy Approach.* Brunner/Mazel, Inc. New York.

Moss, H. and Damasio, A. R. (2001). 'Emotion, cognition, and the human brain'. *New York Academy of Sciences*, www.SeeMe.ie 935, 98–100.

Part Two: Anxiety and Depression

2. Anxiety

Barry, H. P. (2009). *Flagging the Therapy: Pathways out of Depression and Anxiety.* Liberties Press Dublin.

Barry, H. P. (2016). *Anxiety and Panic: How to Reshape your Anxious Mind and Brain.* Liberties Press Dublin.

Barry, H. P. (2017). *Emotional Resilience: How to Safeguard your Mental Health.* Orion Spring.

Bukalo, O., Courtney, R. P., Silverstein, S., Brehm, C., Hartley, N. D. and Whittle, N. et al (2015). 'Prefrontal inputs to the amygdala instruct fear extinction memory formation'. *Sci. Adv.* 1, e1500251.

Handley, A. K., Egan S. J., Kane R. T. and Rees C. S. (2014). 'The relationships between perfectionism, pathological worry and generalised anxiety disorder'. *BMC Psychiatry* 14:98.

LeDoux, J. E. (2015). *Anxious: using the brain to understand and treat fear and anxiety.* New York: Viking.

LeDoux, J. E. (2008). 'Amygdala'. *Scholarpedia*, 3(4):2698.

LeDoux J. E. (2003). 'The emotional brain, fear, and the amygdala', *Cellular and Molecular Neurobiology*, 23, Nos. 4/5.

Murphy. E. (2013). *Five Steps to Happiness.* Dublin.

Pittman, C. M and Karle, E. M. (2015). *Rewire your anxious brain.* New Harbinger Publications Inc. California.

Reinecke, A., Thilo, K., Filippini, N., Croft, A. and Harmer, C. J. (2014). 'Predicting rapid response to cognitive-behavioural treatment for panic disorder: the role of hippocampus, insula, and dorsolateral prefrontal cortex.' *Behav. Res. Ther.* 62: 120–8.

Reinecke, A., Waldenmaier, L., Cooper, M. J. and Harmer, C. J. (2014). 'Changes in automatic threat processing precede and predict clinical changes with exposure-based cognitive-behaviour therapy for panic disorder'. *Biol. Psychiatry,* 73 (11): www.SeeMe.ie 1064–70.

3. Depression

Barry, H. P. (2009). *Flagging the Therapy: Pathways out of Depression and Anxiety.* Liberties Press Dublin.

Barry, H. P. (2012). *Depression: A Practical Guide.* Liberties Press Dublin.

Barry, H. P. (2017). *Emotional Resilience: How to Safeguard your Mental Health.* Orion Spring.

Barry, H. P. (2018). *Self-Acceptance: How to Banish the Self-Esteem Myth, Accept Yourself Unconditionally and Revolutionize your Mental Health.* Orion Spring.

Carhart-Harris, R. L., Roseman, L., Bolstridge, M., et al. (2017). 'Psilocybin for treatment-resistant depression: fMRI-measured brain mechanisms.' *Sci Rep.* 7(1):13187.

Daniel, J. and Haberman, M. (2018). 'Clinical potential of psilocybin as a treatment for mental health conditions.' *Ment. Health Clin.* 7(1):24–28.

Hamilton, J. P., Farmer, M., Fogelman, P. and Gotlib, I. H. (2015). 'Depressive Rumination, The Default-Mode Network, and The Dark Matter of Neuroscience'. *Biol. Psychiatry,* 78 (4): 224–30.

Kaltenboeck, A. and Harmer, C. (2018). 'The neuroscience of depressive disorders: A brief review of the past and some considerations about the future.' *Brain and Neuroscience Advances*, 2: 1–6.

Lapidus, K. A., Levitch, C. F., Perez, A. M., et al. (2014). 'A randomized controlled trial of intranasal ketamine in major depressive disorder.' *Biol Psychiatry*, 76:970–6.

Lyons, T., Carhart-Harris, R. L. (2018). 'More Realistic Forecasting of Future Life Events After Psilocybin for Treatment-Resistant Depression.' *Front Psychol.* 9:1721.

Romeo, B., Choucha, W., Fossati P. et al. (2015). 'Meta-analysis of short- and mid-term efficacy of ketamine in unipolar and bipolar depression.' *Psychiatry Res.* 23:682–8.

Schwartz, J., Murrough, J. W. and Iosifescu, D. V. (2016). 'Ketamine for treatment-resistant depression: recent developments and clinical applications.' *Evidence-Based Mental Health*, 19:35–38.

Zhu, X. et al. (2017). 'Rumination and Default Mode Network Subsystems Connectivity in First-episode, Drug-Naïve Young Patients with Major Depressive Disorder'. *Scientific reports*, 7:43105.

Part Three: Shame and Guilt

4. Shame

Barry, H. P. (2018). *Self-Acceptance: How to Banish the Self-Esteem Myth, Accept Yourself Unconditionally and Revolutionize your Mental Health*. Orion Spring.

Candea, D. and Szentagotai, M. (2013). 'Shame and psychopathology: from research to clinical practice'. *Journal of*

Cognitive and Behavioral Psychotherapies, 13 (1), 97–109.

Cunningham, K. C., LoSavio, S. T., Dennis P. A., et al. (2019). 'Shame as a mediator between posttraumatic stress disorder symptoms and suicidal ideation among veterans.' *J Affect Disorder*, 15(243):216–219.

Hack, J. and Martin, J. (2018). 'Expressed Emotion, Shame, and Non-Suicidal Self-Injury.' *Int. J. Environ. Res. Public Health*, 15(5), 890.

Leary, M. R. (2015). 'Emotional responses to interpersonal rejection.' *Dialogues in clinical neuroscience*, 17(4), 435–441.

Miceli, M. and Castelfranchi, C. (2018). 'Reconsidering the Differences Between Shame and Guilt.' *Europe's Journal of Psychology*, 14(3), 710–733.

Velotti, P., Garofalo, C., Bottazzi F., & Caretti, V. (2017). 'Faces of Shame: Implications for Self-Esteem, Emotion Regulation, Aggression, and Well-Being.' *Journal of Psychology*, 151:2, 171–184.

5. Guilt

Miceli, M., & Castelfranchi, C. (2018). 'Reconsidering the Differences Between Shame and Guilt.' *Europe's Journal of Psychology*, 14(3), 710–733.

Shen, L. (2018). 'The evolution of shame and guilt.' *PLoS ONE* 13(7).

Leary, M. R. (2015). 'Emotional responses to interpersonal rejection.' *Dialogues in clinical neuroscience*, 17(4), 435–441.

Part Four: Hurt and Anger

6. Hurt

Barry, H. P. (2017). *Emotional Resilience: How to Safeguard your Mental Health.* Orion Spring.

Tchalova, K., and Eisenberger, N. I. (2015). 'How the Brain Feels the Hurt of Heartbreak: Examining the Neurobiological Overlap Between Social and Physical Pain.' In: Arthur W. Toga, editor. *Brain Mapping: An Encyclopaedic Reference,* 3: 15–20. Academic Press: Elsevier

Leary, M. R. (2015). 'Emotional responses to interpersonal rejection.' *Dialogues in clinical neuroscience,* 17(4), 435–441.

7. Anger

Batrinos, M. L. (2012). 'Testosterone and aggressive behaviour in man.' *International Journal of Endocrinology and Metabolism,* 10(3), 563–568. doi:10.5812/ijem.3661.

Peterson, C. K. and Harmon-Jones, E. (2012). 'Anger and Testosterone: Evidence That Situationally-Induced Anger Relates to Situationally-Induced Testosterone.' *Emotion,* 12(5):899–902.

Part Five: Grief

8. Grief

Buckley, T., McKinley, S., Tofler, G., Bartrop R. (2010). 'Cardiovascular risk in early bereavement: a literature review and proposed mechanisms.' *Int J Nurs Stud.* 47(2):229–238.

Brown, L. K. and Brown, M. (1998). *When Dinosaurs Die: A Guide to Understanding Death (Dino Life Guides for Families).* Little, Brown Books for Young Readers.

Bibliography

Bonanno, G. A. (2009). *The other side of sadness: What the new science of bereavement tells us about life after loss.* Basic Books New York.

Bonanno, G. A. (2004). 'Loss, Trauma, and Human Resilience: Have We Underestimated the Human Capacity to Thrive After Extremely Aversive Events?'. *American Psychologist*, 59(1): 20–8.

Carey, I. M., Shah, S. M., DeWilde, S., Harris, T., Victor, C. R., Cook, D. G. (2014). 'Increased Risk of Acute Cardiovascular Events After Partner Bereavement: A Matched Cohort Study'. *JAMA Intern Med.*174(4):598–605.

Guldin, M. B. et al. (2017). 'Risk of suicide, deliberate self-harm and psychiatric illness after the loss of a close relative: A nationwide cohort study'. *World Psychiatry: Official Journal of the World Psychiatric Association (WPA)* 16(2): 193–199.

Knowles, L. M., Ruiz, J. M., O'Connor, M. F. (2019). 'A Systematic Review of the Association Between Bereavement and Biomarkers of Immune Function'. *Psychosomatic Medicine*: 81 (5): 415–433.

Kubler-Ross, E. (1969). *On Death and Dying.* Macmillan New York.

Kubler-Ross, E., and Kestler, D. (2005). 'On Grief and Grieving: Finding the Meaning of Grief Through the Five Stages of Loss'.

MacIejewski, P. K., Zhang, B., Block, S. D., Prigerson, H. G. (2007). 'An Empirical Examination of the Stage Theory of Grief'. *JAMA: The Journal of the American Medical Association*, 297 (7): 716–23.

Moon, R., Kondo, N., Glymour, M. M., Subramanian, S. V. (2011). 'Widowhood and mortality: a meta-analysis'. *PLoS One*, 6(8).

Stroebe, M. et al. (2017). 'Cautioning Health-Care Professionals.' *Omega vol.* 74(4): 455–473.

Rubin, S. S. (1999). 'The two-track model of bereavement: overview, retrospect, and prospect'. *Death Studies*, 23(8):681–714.

Schonfeld, D. J., Demaria, T. and Committee on Psychosocial Aspects of Child and Family Health, Disaster Preparedness Advisory Council. (2016) 'Supporting the Grieving Child and Family'. *Paediatrics*, 138(3), e2016–2147.

Vitlic, A. et al. (2014). 'Bereavement reduces neutrophil oxidative burst only in older adults: role of the HPA axis and immunesenescence.' *Immunity & Ageing: I & A*, 11(13).

INDEX

Index

Index

burial, grief and 185–6

cardiovascular system 181–2
CBT (Cognitive Behaviour
  Therapy) 23–8
  anger 155–65
  anxiety 38–45, 47–8, 54–5
  depression 62–5, 81, 83–91
  grief and
    loss of child 260–72
    loss of parent 241–7
    loss of partner 227–36
  guilt 118–25
  hurt and 136–47
  shame 102–11
child, coping with the death of a
  248–72
  coping emotionally 249–53
  suicide 253–72
clinical depression *see* Depression
  (clinical illness)
Cognitive Behaviour Therapy
  (CBT) 23–8
  anger 155–65
  anxiety 38–45, 47–8, 54–5
  depression 62–5, 81, 83–91
  grief and
    loss of child 260–72
    loss of parent 241–7
    loss of partner 227–36
  guilt 118–25
  hurt and 136–47
  shame 102–11

Coin Exercise 56, 69
concentration, reduced 74–5
'consequences' (C in ABC model)
  anger 155–65
  anxiety 38–45, 47–8, 54–5
  definition 25
  depression 62–5, 83–91
  grief and
    loss of child 260–72
    loss of parent 241–7
    loss of partner 227–36
  guilt 118–25
  hurt and 136–47
  phobias 27, 42–5
  shame 102–11
crying 187–8, 196–7, 224, 227,
  260–1, 265

death *see* grief
debt 97
Default – Mode Network (DMN)
  78–9
denial, grief and 172
Depression (clinical illness)
  definition 59
  the illness 71–2
  Major Depression (MDD) 71–9
depression (emotion) 59–91
  definition 8–9
  the emotion 60–61
  exercises 68–70
  grief and 172, 179, 201–2,
    239–40

Index

Index

RESOURCES

Self-Help Groups

Anxiety UK

Anxiety UK is a national registered charity formed in 1970 to provide help for anyone affected by anxiety, stress and anxiety based depression. The website maintains an up-to-date list of independent, verified self-help groups located across the UK and provides a wealth of self-help resources online.

Helpline: 03444 775 774

support@anxietyuk.org.uk | www.anxietyuk.org.uk

Aware

Aware is a voluntary organisation established in 1985 to support those experiencing depression and their families. Aware endeavours to create a society where people with mood disorders and their families are understood and supported, and to obtain the resources to enable them to defeat depression. Weekly support group meetings at approximately fifty locations nationwide, including Northern Ireland, offer peer support and provide factual information, and enable people to gain the skills they need to help them cope with depression. Aware's 'Beat the Blues' educational programme is run in secondary schools.

Helpline: 1800 80 48 48 (Ireland only)
supportmail@aware.ie | www.aware.ie

ChildLine

ChildLine, a service run by the ISPCC, seeks to empower and support children using the medium of telecommunications and information technology. The service is designed for all children and young people up to the age of eighteen in Ireland.

Helpline: 0800 1111 (UK)
www.childline.org.uk

Grow

Established in Ireland in 1969, GROW is Ireland's largest mutual-help organisation in the area of mental health. It is anonymous, nondenominational, confidential and free. No referrals are necessary. GROW aims to achieve self-activation through mutual help. Its members are enabled, over time, to craft a step-by-step recovery or personal-growth plan, and to develop leadership skills that will help others.

Helpline: 1 890 474 474 (Ireland only)
info@grow.ie | www.grow.ie

Mind

Mind is one of the UK's leading mental health charities. The organisation has been committed to making sure that mental health advice and support is accessible for anyone who needs it. In 2013 the charity successfully campaigned against the Mental Health (Discrimination) Act, removing the last significant forms of discrimination that prevented people with mental health problems from serving on a jury, being a director of a company or serving as an MP. With over 375,000 local Minds across England and Wales, the charity provides millions with services that include supported housing, crisis helplines, drop-in centres, employment and training schemes, counselling, peer support, information and befriending.

Helpline: 0300 123 3393
www.mind.org.uk

No Panic

No Panic is a charity which aims to facilitate the relief and rehabilitation of people suffering from panic attacks, phobias, obsessive compulsive disorders and other related anxiety disorders, including tranquilliser withdrawal, and to provide support to sufferers and their families and carers. Founded by Colin M. Hammond in the UK, this group has extended its activities to Ireland, where it is organised by therapist Caroline McGuigan.

Helpline: 0844 967 4848
Youth Helpline: 0330 606 174
info@nopanic.org.uk | nopanic.org.uk

Samaritans

Samaritans was started in 1953 in London by a young vicar called Chad Varah; the first branch in the Republic of Ireland opened in Dublin in 1970. Samaritans provides a twenty-four-hour-a-day confidential service offering emotional support for people who are experiencing feelings of distress or despair, including those which may lead to suicide.

Helpline: 116 123
jo@samaritans.org | www.samaritans.org

Sane

Established in 1986 to improve the quality of life for all those affected by mental health problems, SANE is a UK-wide charity with three main objectives: to raise awareness and combat stigma about mental illness; to provide emotional support and care; to aid research into the causes and treatments of serious mental health conditions such as schizophrenia and depression. SANE provides confidential emotional support, information and access to self-management strategies.

Helpline: 0300 304 7000
info@sane.org.uk | www.sane.org.uk

ACKNOWLEDGEMENTS

I would like to start, as always, by thanking my editorial team at Orion UK for all their wonderful assistance in publishing this book. I want to especially thank my editor, Pippa Wright, who has been so supportive, guiding me patiently along the right path in relation to this book. I am also indebted as always to Ru Merritt, for her assistance and patience in bringing it all together. I would also like to thank publicist Francesca Pearce at Orion UK and publicity director Elaine Egan and Siobhan Tierney from Hachette Ireland for their assistance in the PR, sales and marketing areas.

I also owe a huge debt of gratitude as always to Vanessa Fox O'Loughlin, my agent, who has made this project possible.

I would like to especially thank my dear friend and colleague Dr Muiris Houston of *The Irish Times*, for taking the time to review the text, and for his friendship and support. His reports in the excellent Health Plus supplement are respected by us all.

I send the warmest of thanks as always to my good friend Cathy Kelly (bestselling author and UNICEF ambassador) for her constant kindness and support throughout the years. I am also indebted to my friend and national treasure, Sr Stan, founder of Focus Ireland and The Sanctuary, who embodies what emotional healing is all about.

I am also indebted to the eminent Professor Ian Robertson,

Professor of Psychology, Trinity College Dublin and psychologist Fiona Doherty for taking the time to review the script and for their support and encouragement.

I am, as always, indebted to my friend and colleague Enda Murphy for his invaluable assistance. A brilliant CBT therapist and former ICGP tutor who has taught me much of what I know, I am deeply grateful for his support and insightful comments. We share a joint vision of where mental health should be moving towards. We both value our national radio slot on *Today with Sean O'Rourke* very highly, and I would like to take this opportunity to thank Sean (a true gentleman of Irish media) and his wonderful team, particularly Cora Ennis and series producer Tara Campbell, for allowing us the opportunity to highlight key areas of mental health. A special thanks to other members of the team, especially Alistair Mc Connell, Geraldine Collins, Mary O'Hagan, among many others, for their constant support over the years.

I am deeply indebted as always to my colleague, Professor Catherine Harmer, Professor of Cognitive Neuroscience, Oxford, for her support and for taking time out of her busy schedule to review this work.

I would also like to thank Bruce Daisley, former vice president of Twitter Europe and bestselling author, for also kindly agreeing to review the script and for his warm words. It was much appreciated. I also must send the warmest of thanks to *Sunday Independent* columnist Niamh Horan for all of her support and for reviewing the manuscript.

I am honoured that friend and colleague Senator Joan Freeman, former Chairperson of the Joint Oireachtas Committee on the Future of Mental Health and who has done so much for suicide prevention in Ireland and USA, took time out to review it.

I am also so appreciative to my international colleagues

Acknowledgements

Professor Ray Lam, University of British Columbia, Canada, and Professor Larry Culpepper, Boston University, USA, both of whom have been so supportive and for taking the time to review this book.

A special thank you to Oliver Doonan and Joseph Ryan who allowed me the honour of dedicating this book to their sons, who both died by suicide, and for their support and encouragement.

I say a special thanks to my sons Daniel and Joseph (and his wife Sue and my beautiful granddaughter Saoirse) and to my daughter Lara, her husband Hans (and my two much loved grandsons Ciaran and Sean) for all their love and support and for keeping me well grounded!

As always, I reserve my biggest 'thank you' to my wife Brenda, whose love, friendship, support, encouragement and particularly patience has made this book and indeed the whole series possible. You will always have my back as I have yours. You are my light in the darkness, and truly my soulmate. '*Mo ghra, mo chroi.*' (My love, my heart.)

ABOUT THE AUTHOR

Dr Harry Barry is a highly respected Irish author and medic, with over three decades of experience as a GP. With a keen interest in the area of mental health and suicide prevention, Dr Barry is the author of numerous books addressing various aspects of mental health including anxiety, depression, toxic stress and emotional resilience.

A practical guide teaching you how to best tackle life's challenges.

'Another masterpiece from a cutting-edge expert'
Dr Muiris Houston,
The Irish Times

EMOTIONAL
RESILIENCE

How to safeguard your
mental health

THE BRAND NEW BOOK FROM
INTERNATIONAL BESTSELLING AUTHOR
DR HARRY BARRY

A practical guide to identifying and managing stress.

TOXIC
STRESS

A step-by-step guide
to managing stress

DR HARRY BARRY

S

A practical guide exploring the role of therapy in depression and anxiety.

FLAGGING THE
THERAPY

Pathways out of
depression and anxiety

DR HARRY BARRY

S

A practical guide to understanding and coping with anxiety, depression, addiction and suicide.

FLAGGING THE PROBLEM

A new approach to mental health

DR HARRY BARRY

S

A practical, four step programme to help you
understand and cope with depression.

DEPRESSION

A practical guide

DR HARRY BARRY

S

A practical guide to understanding, managing and overcoming anxiety and panic attacks.

ANXIETY
AND PANIC

How to reshape your
anxious mind and brain

DR HARRY BARRY

S